The Bullet Ship

Living Courageously in a Sea of Fear

Roi Ostrovsky

info@roi.pub

www.Roi.Pub

ISBN 978-965-92661-0-4

Disclaimer:

The contents of this book are a sole expression and opinion of its author, and it is designed for informational purposes only. Neither the publisher nor the author shall be liable for any physical, psychological, emotional, financial, or commercial damages, including but not limited to special, incidental, consequential, or other damages. The physical exercises and activities described here may be too strenuous for some people, and the reader(s) should consult a physician before engaging in them.

To my loving family, friends, and everybody
who is a part of my journey.

Elliott Hulse, I thank you for mentoring me along my way
and teaching me invaluable lessons.

All of you made this book possible.

A ship in harbor is safe,
but that is not what ships are built for.

—John A. Shedd

Claim Your Free Gift

Hello and congratulations for picking up The Bullet Ship!

One of my goals with The Bullet Ship is to help you unleash the primal force that's treasured inside your body. This is the purpose of Part Four of this book.

But words aren't enough.

This is why I crafted a special video that will guide you, step by step, in unlocking your body's energy and aggression.

To get the video, please go to www.Roi.Pub/Gift and follow the instructions.

I wish you an enjoyable reading and great results.

Roi Ostrovsky

Table of Contents

Introduction

In this book I'm going to share with you the lessons I learned along my journey about how I went from being the depressed, self-doubting, lost kid I was in my school days to being the courageous, risk-taking, happy man that I am today.

I used to hate everybody, including myself. I was getting picked on by bullies and had almost no friends; for years this was the world I lived in. I thought that it was everybody else's fault that I was insecure and powerless, and at some point I thought, well, maybe I was destined for depression and isolation. The pain was so deep, and my heart ached so bad at times that thinking about how it would be to end the whole story was simply inevitable. But even when these thoughts possessed my mind, *I knew*, with every cell of my body that I deserved more than this. I would never give up.

I was withdrawn; I went through a serious bout of depression, and I held this position until I was around sixteen. That is when things started to change for me. That is when *I* started to change things for myself.

I understood that my misery had become a safe place, a comforting, cozy blanket to hide behind. I blamed the world, myself, my parents, and my circumstances, but at some point I said; "I just hate this! There has to be more to life than this!"

It took me some time to start the process, but eventually I started working on myself. It was a painful process of waking up, a death and rebirth. I started working hard, twice as hard for every depressed day I experienced. I began going to the gym and disciplining myself—sleep, nutrition, books, everything. I had to! I'd had enough!

That was a long time ago.

Ever since, I've been pushing myself to the extreme. Dawn to dusk, my mission in this universe is to set myself free from the boundaries imposed on me by myself and society so that I can live my dream and help others do the same.

Today I am at a point in my life where I'm so free in just doing me that I feel I must share the secrets that helped me get to this place. There is a fire burning inside of me; I cannot explain how vast it feels. But *I need to share it.* I must.

Goosebumps go through my body as I'm writing these lines.

I have committed myself to living my truth. I have committed to follow my heart, as dangerous as it might be. I might die in the process, but every morning I am filled with exuberance that knows no limits (although if I don't sleep enough, I will wake up tired. I'm still not a superman...)

This truth—yes, truth—has and will set people free from the prison that has been built brick by brick, first by society and now it is being enforced every single day by no one else than you! You were taught it, and now you do it to yourself.

For me, this book is jumping off a cliff. This book represents stepping out in trust and embarking on the journey that my heart was calling me to. It's leaving all the safety and security behind, exposing myself to the world—and most of all, it's dealing with the possibility of failure.

On my journey towards freedom I have made a lot of mistakes. I have also encountered many sources of knowledge—from people to books—that just didn't deliver. This fact made me look and search even harder, first out there and eventually inward.

In this book, I've synthesized everything I have found and learned during the years from my own experience—everything that really helped me and the people around me to dissolve our shells, expose our true fires, and live more passionate and courageous lives.

There's simply too much noise out there, and my aim is to give people the real essence, which is why I wrote this book. I'm not training you to become someone you're not. I'm training you, to be yourself.

I want to you to dissolve your fake mask. I want you to die and be reborn in the process of unleashing your true, courageous, powerful nature.

But I want to give you a heads up. If you came here for promises and easy shortcuts—you will not find them here. Everything in this book has been a result of devotion, bulls' willpower, and patience. You will have to harness these three virtues if you really want to change; no excuses accepted.

Also keep in mind that this is not a linear process, and what changed your friend's life in a matter of weeks could take months or years for you—each individual has his own pace. So don't compare your pace with that of the people around you and get discouraged. Rather use this gap in progress as motivation to keep moving forward and reaching new heights on your pilgrimage.

Absorb this book in its totality, allow some time for things to really kick in, and come back to key chapters often to remind yourself what to do. Use a pen or a marker to highlight what you find most powerful.

Also, jumping from one book to another is the *worst* thing you can do to yourself, because when you have too much information—even when the truth is laid out in front of you—you are unable to spot it. So stick to this book for at least a couple of months before jumping to conclusions.

To women who get their hands on this book—since it was written from my experience as a man, it's first and foremost geared toward men. But I'm sure you will find golden nuggets here too.

I believe in simplicity and directness. This is why this book is quite simple. This is also what makes the content of it so profound.

"I learned that the world has a soul, and that whoever understands that soul can also understand the language of things. I learned that many alchemists realized their Personal Legends, and wound up discovering the Soul of the World, the Philosopher's Stone, and the Elixir of Life. But, above all, I learned that these things are all so simple that they could be written on the surface of an emerald."[1]

"Why Did You Choose This Name?"

It's ten o'clock on a warm, sticky July night. The street lights are beaming fiercely.

I'm sitting in my car, in the parking lot in front of my house.

There's a black bag in the seat next to me.

Inside, there's a wrapped present, a late twentieth birthday gift.

My best friend, the person with whom I share my journey, got it for me.

---

[1] Paulo Cohelo, *The Alchemist* (New York: HarperCollins Publishing, 1993)

I was at his house an hour earlier when he gave it to me. After handing it to me, he looked into my eyes and said with a smile:

"Don't open it up here, man; wait until you're alone."

I had to hold myself from just tearing the whole thing apart.

That's it. It's time. Finally I get to tear it and see what's inside.

I open it up.

And inside I see a ship.

A big, golden, heavy metallic ship.

Made out of bullets? Seriously?

I try to find an explanation inside the bag. A card, an I-didn't-know-what-to-get note, something!

Abyss.

I get out of the car and start heading home...

Here I am, walking home with a bullet ship, a black bag, and a confused face.

When I get home, I check the bag one last time before disposing of it.

There's a note! I probably missed it because of the darkness.

It is a rolled sheet of paper, held by a small blue ribbon.

I slowly untie the ribbon... excited by what I might find.

One quote broke the night's silence.

"A ship in harbor is safe, but that is not what ships are built for."[2]

What Is Confidence?

Forget everything you thought you knew about Confidence.

The term Confidence is very shallow, and to really make a change, you must first redefine it. When you think of someone who is confident, you think of an image. You ignore the fact that he's a human, and just like every other human - he has shortcomings as well. Confidence is an image, simply because it is superficial and has unrealistic expectations attached to it. On the other hand, Courage is intrinsic and grounded. It's real. It's humane.

People define *confidence* by looking at the people who are the most powerful—those with money, status, or looks. But you see, most of these people are just wearing fake masks that give them power. Fake Power. They live through their pumped up egos.

These people might look and sound powerful, but underneath this rigid layer they are soft as butter. A sheep in a wolf's body... A bird who roars like a tiger.

And it goes the other way around too. In the same way they are wearing a mask, so do you. Maybe you're feeling not so confident and courageous—you are a wolf in a sheep's body, a tiger who's chirping like a bird.

I, too, thought for years that money, good looks, or social status were the root of confidence. For some reason—I'll call it reality—I encountered many people that fit this profile, but for most of them, as soon as you touched a small button, they broke and unveiled a fragile, defensive person. As time went by, and I met more people

---

[2] John A. Shedd, *Salt From My Attic* (Portland: Mosher Press, 1928)

like this—beautiful, smart, or rich—it became more and more apparent that their muscles, knowledge, and Ferraris were just a charade. A persona. It covered pain, wounds, and puss. Loads of it. You take their cars away from them, shave their heads, or make them mail-room workers instead of CEOs, and sheep with helpless looks in their eyes will appear in no time.

True confidence means *being courageous*. It simply means letting your heart carry you into the unknown. It's allowing yourself to be the crazy, genuine, imperfect human being that you are, and accepting your flaws in their entirety. Without denial, judgment, or pretending.

People who are truly confident are the ones who don't try to suppress their true natures so that their behavior will fit into the little box created by society. Confident people might still be afraid at times, and they might tremble and shiver with fear—just like any other human being—but they accept their wide range of emotions and aren't afraid of expressing them.

They live by their own terms and define their own rules. They refuse to suppress their true natures to satisfy someone else. In essence, that's confidence. That simple, yet at the same time, it's so challenging!

Real confidence is a result of courage. It's not a mask. Courage is who you are. So our purpose here is not to create a new confident persona that will take the place of your old insecure one, but to dissolve both of these fakes and to find your true core. To dissolve both in the potion of courage.

Part 1

**Only Two Ingredients
for True Confidence**

Chapter 1

Acknowledge Your Shit

> In the long run, we shape our lives, and we shape ourselves. The process never ends until we die. And the choices we make are ultimately our own responsibility.
>
> —Eleanor Roosevelt

Responsibility is the first step toward confidence and freedom.

Just think about this crazy concept for one moment: if every problem in your life is up to you to solve—this means you have the power and freedom to choose whether you're going to live with it or not. Fix it, or leave it as it is—it's in your hands. The sword that you gave away years ago as a child who spat out the strained peas Mom was trying to put into your mouth, and got scolded for it, comes back to its rightful owner. *You* are now in control.

Start taking responsibility for your situation! Yes, there is a decent chance that as a child you acquired your low levels of confidence and self-esteem because of your abusive parents and environment... but it all happened years ago. Carve these words deep into your consciousness; today, *now*, as a grown human being, you are The Master of Your Own Destiny.

Every time you think that someone else is responsible for what you are feeling, you give away your personal power, and instead of harnessing the pain and anger you feel to create a change in your life, to exhibit a warrior's characteristics, you choose to be a victim.

Sure, it's convenient to blame others. You create a fiction in your mind in which someone else is crucified for your problems. In reality, you are the one crucified for your problems; you just choose to turn your head away from this fact—thus you lose very precious time not fulfilling your potential.

Some people don't take responsibility out of pure blindness. They just don't know that they are free underneath years of imprisonment. But there is another group of people that goes even deeper down the rabbit hole, and after discovering that they have full control over their lives, they choose to continue to live by their old patterns. You will be different. I know it.

It's common for me to meet people that ask for my help, and even after they understand logically and emotionally that they are digging their own holes—they just leave it as it is. They want a better life but refuse to devote themselves to the process. They will throw any amount of money, but won't pay the price of hard work. If you are going to do this, stop reading now, and ask for a refund. I mean it.

Each and every human being, including you, knows deep within that he's responsible for his situation, but taking responsibility is probably harder than any other step in the process of changing your life. This is the step where you cut the excuses and grow up to become a man, one who takes initiative.

Stop Being Full of Shit

One excuse I often hear from people who are considering a change in their life is: "well, my life isn't that bad..."

I call bullshit.

If you were happy with your situation, you wouldn't have had to wake up miserable every day. If you were happy, your life would have been more exciting and adventurous. If you were happy, you would have had less anxiety about work and more anxiety about how exciting and spontaneous your life was.

If you were happy... you wouldn't have been reading this book.

We put on many different kinds of excuses and faces to mask who we are and what we truly feel about *everything*. I mean, what else can you do if the only thing you are taught is to put on a smile, never rock the goddamn boat, and sit on it quietly, letting the water carry you to your death?

Another very popular excuse is: "it's just not the right time..."

Come on, seriously. I don't even want to write this paragraph! This excuse is the one I just hate the most. Aren't you fed up? Aren't you tired of living a mediocre life? Haven't you had enough of not being able to stand up for yourself?

I know that deep down you are on fire! You just can't wait to storm into your boss's office and tell him, "I deserve a raise. I earned it." Or to approach this girl you have had a crush on for so long and tell him or her: "You and me, tonight, at eight o'clock; the only option is yes."

The right time will never come—there's simply no such thing. If you sit with your arms crossed waiting for power, courage, balls, God, or paying of your debt—your whole life will pass by you. I've met people who are sixty and have postponed living because they were always too busy... always too busy thinking "why it's not the right time". They're everywhere, and they are miserable.

Someday is today. Stop wasting time! Stop waiting for the power! "The law of nature is, Do the thing, and you shall have the power."[3] Ralph Waldo Emerson knew, that waiting for the power won't grant him it. By going into the arena, you find the powers... even if at first you thought you don't have them.

You need to be aware of your own excuses. I gave here only two, but there are infinite variations, and all of them, doesn't matter how logical and reasonable they seem—are traps. Humans have a tendency to find thousands of reasons why they can't when there's sweat involved.

So you can keep telling yourself stories and suffer with no return, or you can cut the crap by acknowledging that you're responsible—and start getting rewards for your suffering.

Just imagine! Being able to approach a girl on the bus, dancing on the street by yourself completely freely, or just taking the next plane to Paris for the sake of the adventure; wouldn't it be great?

All of this and much more is possible for the one who is courageous, and the first step on your journey to the summit begins with taking responsibility.

Now, I know that responsibility is a concept that is hard to bear at first. It was for me too. But if you are dedicated to breaking free from society's shackles, taking responsibility is a must.

---

[3] Ralph Waldo Emerson, *Essays: First Series, Compensation* (1841)

Take Responsibility Now!

I don't care what your story is. I don't care how hard it is. I don't care, and neither should you, not anymore. The people who are stuck in the past are the ones who drag themselves out of bed, are satisfied by mediocrity, and wake up every morning knowing exactly what awaits them.

Today, *now*, you must answer a simple question that will determine the rest of your life. I decided to write this part early to filter the people who read this book. I want people who want to be reborn. I'm not playing.

The question is this: are you willing to acknowledge that everything in your life is up to you to change?

I want you to ask yourself this question in a tone that will resonate deep into your core. Put aside your nice fake story, get in touch with your pain, and answer this honestly. The answer to this question will determine whether you choose to take responsibility, and grab the reins of your life back to your hands, or choose to forgo your responsibility, and leave the reins to those around you to control you.

Now get a smooth sheet of paper. Write down the date, day, and time.

On this sheet of paper, write honestly about your life. Don't filter, and don't exaggerate; simply capture your daily life on paper, write everything as it is. All of it. How confident are you feeling? How are your relationships going? How is your career? Are you happy with your situation? What feeling are you carrying with you most in your life? What is your dream? Who are you blaming for your situation? How hungry you are to change your life?

Write a letter to yourself. I want you to dig deep into your pain and wounds, and uncover the truth. Hold nothing back; let the words flow.

This is not some new-age self-help letter. This is a statement, a call to action.

Finished? Good! Now read it from top to bottom.

As you are reading it, I want you to look at your situation and *hate it.* I want you to despise it, hate it with every cell of your body. I want you to feel anger flowing through you, generating an electrifying wave of energy.

I want you to feel like this shit is over—no more living like this, no more bullshit, no more games. This time you are taking control of your life.

Say to yourself out loud, "I DESERVE A GREAT LIFE!"

Under the letter you wrote, I want you to write down a commitment to yourself. Commit to change. Write down, "It's up to me to change my life! I'm taking full responsibility over my life, and I will slay my dragons."

Write it in big capital letters without boundaries; write outside of the lines! Make it huge! Scream if you have to; throw the pen on the floor and break it afterward; take a pillow and scream into it; punch the wall!

Feel the winds of change coming in; the true you emerges from within and washes you, like a cool breeze on a sunny day; feel how the mask you've been wearing for so long, fear and mediocrity fade into ashes.

Now flip this sheet of paper. This time, you are going to write the opposite; you are going to express your dream. Write everything you believe you deserve, in every area of your life—confidence, relationships, job, income, happiness... and be as descriptive as possible. What will you enjoy when you'll be more confident? What the relationship of your dreams looks like? What about the job of your dreams? Don't filter or limit yourself, and let the words come from deep within your heart...

Now close your eyes, and with deep breathes, imagine everything you wrote down as vividly as possible... imagine as if right now you already have the relationship of your dreams, the job, the income... the confidence! Listen to the sounds, absorb the scenes and the smells... let the feelings flow through your heart.

Now sign your name at the bottom. This letter is now your anchor, keep it somewhere safe, and come back to it often. Understand that everything you dream of is achievable; it's only a matter of first taking responsibility on what's written on the opposite side, and then taking action toward change.

Our journey is about to begin, I hope you are ready.

Chapter 2

Become Courageous

The secret to happiness is freedom... And the secret to freedom is courage.

　　—Thucydides

So you've acknowledged your shit. I'm proud of you; it takes a lot of courage.

The next step is having the courage to follow your heart—the courage to take action toward changing your life.

Deep down within, each and every one of us has a powerful, blood-pumping machine that's filled with dreams, desires, loves, hates, and all kinds of nurturing and destructive forces of nature.

And it pisses me off to say that we've become such a mind-driven society that your innate, most powerfully dark passions and desires have to be stuffed down... Every time a spontaneous feeling floats up, instead of acting on it, you first completely dissect it in your mind. Only after every possible outcome has been considered, and you've determined that you will not cause social friction and can stay within your comfort zone, are you willing to act. Otherwise you won't make a single step.

Taking a leap of faith, going up to that stunning brunette girl, or looking deep into your coworker's eyes and saying, "I will not take your shit anymore"—no way!

Do you know why?

Because following your heart is dangerous, and that's why you are so attached to certainty and to your mind. Your mind is holding you back, making you stagnate in mediocrity. It will deceive you into believing that it's better to stay there and that you have no power over it.

When you follow your heart, you embrace the unknown, which may hold both physical and mental danger. Now guess what your mind fears the most? You getting hurt. This is why your mind is so afraid of the unknown and will try *everything* to prevent you from going in there, and facing the darkness. The unknown will sometimes make you feel embarrassed. At times the bittersweet taste of being an outcast will be present too. But at the same time, you will feel freedom and exuberance. There's no other way around it if you want to achieve courage and freedom.

See, your mind is supposed to protect you from dangers, help you survive in a society, and allow you to fit in. But here's the catch: when it takes you over, fears come in; you start going against every primordial urge and denying what's in your heart. You then start suffering, living a life that was designed for you by someone else. All self-exploration, adventure, and danger are taken out of the equation...

Your current life is expectable—it maybe dissatisfying, but it provides a comforting illusion of safety and certainty! Following your heart will shake up the ship of your life and stir up the water under you. You will be exposed to more danger, and your reality will change immensely. It's scary, but if you really think about it, what's the worth of a life without danger, without uncertainty? The only ones who experience no danger and uncertainty are those in the graveyard. So when you live your life in a routine and avoid every possible unknown outcome—you become a walking dead, just like every other person you see on the bus on your way to work.

Here is a powerful quote by a powerful man: "The very basic core of a man's living spirit is his passion for adventure. The joy of life comes from our encounters with new experiences, and hence there is no greater joy than to have an endlessly changing horizon, for each day to have a new and different sun."[4]

Chris McCandless knew very deeply, that a human being is most alive not when he's in the safest position possible, but rather when his primordial inclination toward adventure is being fulfilled.

The ones who follow their hearts eat the juiciest apples, breathe the freshest air, and live the best lives. Period.

It's sure as hell not because of the rewards (which hold their own value) that I believe every human being should follow his heart, but it's simply because there is no substitute for the feeling of integrity and fulfillment you get when following your heart. Like a cold shower on a sunny August day, this feeling washes your body with joy.

Courageous VS. Brave

On the surface, being courageous and being brave look pretty much similar. In reality, they have one very profound difference. Being courageous is letting go in trust. Being brave is *forcing* yourself to let go.

Being courageous means following your heart's desire, like a servant following its master. Being courageous is the same as love, a river, or a child who puts his hands in the fire because his heart led him to it. It

---

[4] Christopher Johnson McCandles, Excerpt from a letter (South Dakota: 1992)

may still feel scary and overwhelming, but there's certain serenity when going into the dangerous situation. You embrace this fear and flow with your desire. This is a dance *with* fear. Courage comes by letting go.

But being brave is a mask. It's mental. It roots from your mind.

Brave people stuff their fears down and push themselves to do things they don't want to do. They pretend to be strong and fearless, but deep down they're terrified. Like a skyscraper with lousy foundations or a rootless oak tree... blow some air on it or shake up the ground, and they will come crumbling down like a house made of cards. Brave people go into war even though they're shaking with fear and their hearts call them to do the opposite. This is a dance against fear. Bravery comes by force.

Your ultimate goal should be courage. But to be courageous, you first need to be brave.

I believe bravery has its place, simply because at first you'll have to push yourself into war. You'll have to plow at the beginning, forcing yourself to do hard things you don't necessarily want to do just to get the wheel going and prove to yourself that you actually have the capacity to face your fears. Every time you do something that you're afraid of, even though you're pulled in the other direction, you'll peel away another layer of the armor that's been built around your heart by your safety seeking mind.

After a while of training your ability to plow, you'll become so accustomed to uncertain, discomforting situations that when your heart's true desires arise, you'll be able to act on them instantly, without hesitation, thought, or conscious effort. The action will happen on its own.

When you get to the point of things happening instantly without resistance or the use of force, you will know that you have outgrown bravery and stepped into courage.

Be brave; dive in.

Becoming Courageous Now!

"Live. If you live, God will live with you. If you refuse to run his risks, he'll retreat to that distant heaven and be merely a subject for philosophical speculation. Everyone knows this, but no one takes the first step, perhaps for fear of being called insane."[5]

This is very true. Only when people are willing to risk they start feeling the presence of God among them. But people are too afraid of taking courageous steps, perhaps for the fear of being called insane. So their lives become dry... boring... mechanical.

God, it's a beautiful day.

As I'm sitting at my desk writing this, so many feelings possess my body; I guess that's what rebirth feels like. I have butterflies in my stomach, and I notice every breath. My emotions are flowing in like gushing waterfalls—happiness, sadness, love, passion, hate—you name it.

I was at work when just before closing time, my boss appeared and said to me, "Hey Roi, I've got something you must do! I need it today!"

That meant staying for two more hours after a nine-hour workday.

I mean, I just sighed. I felt completely drained when he told me this. I believe that certain things at work can

---

[5] Paulo Cohelo, *Veronika Decides To Die* (New York: Harper Perennial, 2006)

wait till tomorrow sometimes; and besides, staying meant preventing me from pursuing my personal goals...

But see, for the couple of years that I worked there, every time something like this came up, I stayed—no questions asked.

I was furious about staying, of course, but I just kept on doing it, feeling the flames go through my body ferociously; I wanted to hit my boss! I wanted to throw all these shitty computers the floor, look deep into his black eyes, and say, "I couldn't care less about this job. You do it yourself." And for too long I suppressed this feeling; I denied it.

Staying against my will did enhance a characteristic of mine, to be honest, which is plowing even when I'm tired, and doing my job with all of my heart—regardless of the circumstances. But at that point, plowing had been a part of me for a long time. It became apparent that I had developed a pattern of denying my feelings to please my boss. I was afraid of his reaction. I gave away my personal power in the face of fear.

And now he did it again. He didn't ask; he *told* me to stay.

I felt this heat wave going through my body again, ten times stronger than before, a hundred times stronger.

While my boss is standing in front me, the only thing I could think of was: you will not dictate my life. I knew that *today* was the day.

I packed up my bag, left all my work hanging, came up to my boss, looked him deep in the eyes, and with a deep breath, broke a dead silence saying: "I will not do this, I'm going home."

I turned around, and without waiting for any response, I left.

24

I really can't explain what I felt after taking that step. It was the awakening of the devil. I felt like a beast when a wave of adrenaline rushed through my veins. I felt so alive! I felt like I could do anything... I was the master of my domain. I was in charge. Nobody else was.

The difference between that day and any other day was that I came to realize—in the deepest, most profound way possible—that nobody controls me! Only I decide for myself! I chose to be a rebel. I was done being a sheep.

I can do whatever I want, and people can talk all they want... it doesn't matter. Their talking is simply out there, in the air, and I choose whether to inhale it or not—it doesn't affect me! Understanding this is waking up to the fact that society acts as a scarecrow. But it's just a fucking scarecrow, a wooden doll that's been dressed to look intimidating. Once a bird learns that it had been fooled all along, it can come back and do whatever it wants.

At the end of the day—only you choose what to do and what not to do. Nobody has control over you. You just need to wake yourself up from the dream you've been living in for so long, and courage will flow naturally into your life. You fear going up to your boss—yes, but what's the worst thing that's going to happen? Will you die? And what about the brunette girl on the bus? Can she kill you?

Start looking at all fears as a game. You can't lose!

Stop taking this game too seriously. Whether you approach this girl, go up to your boss, or run naked in the street—you're going to die in fifty years *anyway*. Hell, maybe you'll even die tomorrow. So will I. Start taking risks.

You'll push yourself the first few times, maybe the first few hundred times, but eventually you will learn that no matter how scary and crazy what you did was, it seemed like a dragon in your mind when in reality it was a noisy dog. With time, you will gain the ability to see every action you want to take for what it really is, rather than through the fearful lens of the mind, and that mistakes are impossible. You either succeed, or you learn.

I chose to live by this mantra: "Do the thing you're afraid to do!"

And I know that if you want to win back your lost power and your life, you must recognize what it is in every situation that you really want to do but can't because fear is holding you, and do it anyway. Simple as that, recognize your genuine inclination—and go into the situation, regardless of how scary it is.

Facing your fears is not about feeling confident about going into the situation, and it's not about knowing that it's going to work out; it's about doing it. It's about reclaiming your lost powers and not about the external outcome.

Things may not turn out how you expect them to, but starting today, measure yourself by who you are becoming—and not by what you get.

Embrace this mantra with every cell of your body. I cannot stress enough how powerful and meaningful your life will become because of it. Everything you have ever dreamed of will simply start flowing into your life. You will feel the godly essence of the universe. This is no spiritual, new-age, law-of-attraction kind of thing—you will simply develop the guts to grab what was around you all along.

Part 2

Taking Action

Chapter 3

Turn On the Light

Darkness, does not exist. Darkness, is merely an absence of light.

You can never create or eliminate darkness itself because it doesn't exist. If you want to control the darkness, you will have to do something about the light. Think about it for a moment; when the nighttime comes, it's not that darkness has arrived and made the sun go away—it's the sun that left, and as a result, darkness just appeared to be there.

In the same way, then, fear itself doesn't exist. Fear is a result of lack of trust—it appears *only* when one stops trusting.

When you believe that your heart's desire works against you, that is to say you don't trust it, darkness wins. You start hesitating. An inner conflict arises as the heart pulls toward adventure and danger but the mind pulls toward comfort and safety. Every natural impulse is being stuffed down and analyzed by the mind, as if the heart's desires are the enemy and have to be monitored constantly. This process creates fear and self-doubt.

When you let go and trust in your heart's deepest longings, believe fiercely, and know that eventually things will fall into place—every fear dissolves. The sun comes out...

Fear and self-doubt are burnt off by courage. Remember that.

So don't treat your fear and self-doubt like they're something real because in truth, they are just a result of absence. Your attempts to fight the darkness will result in painful failure and loss of vital energy.

Instead you need to focus on what's real.

When you choose to trust your heart, and you express courage—fear and self-doubt will vanish. Evaporate. The place of darkness will be taken by light.

Just turn on the light.

Chapter 4

The Three-Second Rule

You don't always need a plan!

Think about how our logic has taken us over. Its purpose was to protect us from bears, cars on the road, and people with guns. But when your logic starts to prevent you from doing basically anything that holds a certain danger and discomfort—it becomes quite crazy. It's no longer logic; it's a tyrant, a dictator! And it's very easy to accept it as a reality and live an entire life this way. No doubt, it's a very useful mechanism... but since bears are no longer raiding our streets—I think it's time you start taking more risks, don't you think?

The Three-Second Rule will get you moving and acting on your desires quickly, and will also train you to be more impulsive. Instinctive. It will wake you up from your long-term hibernation. As your courage develops and you follow this rule more, you will suddenly realize that you were able to do everything you dreamed of all along; you just thought about it too much... your mind stood in your way. You will also realize that you have a great capacity to face the unknown and sift your way through it with amazing results.

The idea of this rule is very simple. Act within three seconds from the moment you recognize an inclination toward action. This way, you can act quickly, before your mind goes into gear and blocks you from operating.

For example, I feel like I need to go up to the beautiful woman on the street and ask her out. Three, two, one, go!

Get your foot in the door—figure it out later. That's our motto.

You count to one, and you start moving toward the destination, without a plan or preparation. By creating this momentum, you'll find that stopping is impossible! Once you start moving forward, you will just continue all the way with your mission. Acting within three seconds is like pushing a big rock off a cliff. There's no stopping it.

Now, I know that sometimes it's not that easy to just wake up one day and say, "Boom. Three-second rule. Now." I've been there... It's ok. So to really get the ball going—start doing *everything* within three seconds, no matter how small it seems. For example, you're at home, just chilling on your couch after a long day of work. Suddenly you remember that you need to wash the dishes. *Three, two, one, go!*

You're at work, sitting at your desk and killing time— suddenly you think about how long you've been procrastinating on this desk cleanup. *Three, two, one, go!*

By incorporating this rule into your daily tasks, you will see that going up to a girl and asking for her number is no different than washing the dishes or cleaning up your desk. You'll go from no to yes in a matter of seconds, and you'll kill the excuses and rationalizations at the source. You don't always need a plan...

Chapter 5

Forge Your Soul with Cold Showers

With all the progress that's been made in the last century, it's not hard to understand why people became such cowards. If you really stop and think for a moment, the notion of "The comfier, the better!" got ingrained so deep into our minds that comfort and security became an addiction, making us softer than ever before.

With privileges like air conditioning, cars, abundant food, and comfy shelter, it's very easy to fall prey to this trade-off and lose your capacity to face hardships and discomfort. Think of the cavemen; they had no water heaters and no refrigerators filled with steaks and milk; people worked hard in any weather, under any condition. They used their hands to plow and harvest fields, bathed in freezing lakes, and ran for miles to hunt their dinners. The cavemen were a bunch of badasses with souls forged in fire, razor-sharp minds, and warrior mentalities who could endure fear, discomfort, and pain. But today our culture is too soft! And how can you blame anyone if all this abundance just makes one think, "Well, if all this comfort is available, why should I suffer voluntarily?"

The answer to this question is simple: because, to live a full life—a life of courage and adventure—one has to grow a pair of balls and deal with discomfort; otherwise, that person will live a boring, dull life. And it doesn't matter that your life is already hard—it was chosen *for you*. It's time to actually go into battle *voluntarily* and train your mind and soul because you want to and not because life pulled the sheet out from under you.

One tool that's been in use for many years in Buddhism to build mental endurance and courage is cold water immersions. At first, I tried to look for research and articles—you know, to base my point and prove its authenticity—but then I stopped for a second and wondered *"Prove its authenticity? What is there to prove?"* you see, despite it being true that cold showers benefit your physical health—that's not the point. I'm not introducing you to this technique to make your nose run less during the winter.

What's behind this method is far beyond anything research can prove. The point, the reason why I'm advocating this, is that if you can will yourself to go into an ice-cold shower and stand under the crazy, ass-freezing stream for ten minutes—your mind and soul will turn razor sharp. By taking cold showers, you are deliberately training your ability to face the uncomfortable, and the byproduct of this training is courage. If you can deal with it, you can deal with anything.

Starting today, open every morning with a five-to-ten-minute shower; no hot water allowed! While taking the shower, after the initial shock fades, focus on breathing deeply into your belly and bringing awareness to your body—this will keep you calm and centered in the eye of the storm. Do you think you have the balls for that?

Chapter 6

Learn to Say No!

How many times have you said yes when in reality you wanted to say, "No, fuck off"?

Our society has become way too flaccid and nice. You bend your red lines and your heart's no, way too much to the people around you simply because you're afraid of a little social friction. You're afraid of the confrontation that might arise when you tell someone no.

This subtle, yet very diminishing, characteristic of compliance against your will has created someone who bends down and does things he doesn't want to do in order to please others and avoid confrontation. We have been taught to engage in such behavior since we were little kids. Recall what happened when you misbehaved at school, when you cried and screamed, or when you didn't do what you were supposed to do at work—you were told to sit down, shut up, and do what you are told.

Never disagree. Never raise your voice. That's what we've been taught all along...

So you grew up afraid of saying no. And as time moved on, you did more and more things that enforced this behavior. Now you smile and say yes, but inside you are burning. You hate him, her, them... you hate everybody! You hate your life because you are now doing something you don't want to. You are betraying your inner truth. This is also what causes people to be passive-aggressive. They will smile in your face with the most pleasing attitudes, and inside their hearts they will be wishing that you'll die. Today.

This is the life most people in our society are living. In short, the reason why we're being conditioned to behave in such a manner is because this way it's easy to control us. What would parents do if their children's opinions had the same weight as that of their own? What would schools and governments do if you stood up to your own truth and rebelled against everything that you didn't like? What if every human being followed his inner voice instead of a big book of rules? People would start living, and governments would fall, and nobody wants that, right?

So whenever you notice an inner inclination to decline, but you feel that you're obligated by an unknown force to say yes—decline explicitly.

When you feel like someone, anyone, is doing anything that makes you uncomfortable, don't put up with it. Say *stop*, *no*, or *enough*.

From today on, start taking initiative and standing your own ground. I want you to feel deep inside your body that you're done being a bitch. No one—I mean it, no one—has the right to step on your boundaries unless you permit them. You are in charge! Understand that!

Chapter 7

I-Just-Don't-Want-To Syndrome

At times you will face something I call the *I-just-don't-want-to* syndrome. You will see something challenging, something that deep down you are just craving to do, but in your mind you will think to yourself, "Actually, it's not that I'm afraid or anything; I just don't want to."

These words will sound very convincing in your mind. They will sound true, and you will believe them. Most likely, you will just listen to them, thinking, "Nailed it. I wasn't scared; I simply knew what I wanted." But deep down you'll know it was just a cheap excuse.

Now I don't care how real this excuse might sound to you in your mind. It's an excuse, period. After so many years of living under the shadow cast on you by this excuse, you can't tell when you really don't want to do something or when you're just afraid. There is no distinction right now.

The question I'm about to share with you will reveal your true inclination in any given situation. It will reveal that which lies deep in your heart, underneath your logical rationalizations: "If there was nobody around, would I do it?"

The answer to this question will expose the elephant in the room. A yes means that you are letting others control and dictate your behavior. Yes means that you need to go out and do it. Yes means that for every second you procrastinate, you're betraying yourself.

Before using this simple question, I was the king of I-Don't-Want-To. Really, I could give lectures on why I didn't want to do something. I wanted to approach this beautiful girl with the mini skirt and long legs—but I had more reasons why not to. For years I was avoiding every possibility of facing my fear with this excuse. And truth to be told, although generally I was disappointed with my life; when I used this excuse, I felt good... I felt like this is a valid—not excuse—but rather explanation. That's because our minds have very subtle tricks and traps that go under our radar, but as soon as I started inquiring—I found out that I was deceived quite cleverly... and by no one else than me.

Because at this point of your life, you can't tell the difference between the true and the false; until you feel like you are the master of your fears, you don't have the privilege to say, "I don't want to."

Nobody around, would you do it?

Chapter 8

Damned If You Do, Damned If You Don't

In every single situation where you face a dilemma, you must understand one simple thing: you're fucked either way. Whether you choose to say yes or no, each choice has its own gains and losses.

For example, you face a situation where you want to come up to your boss and ask for a raise, which is a serious matter by all means. Now on the one hand, you are afraid, and you feel like this is too much for you to deal with, so you say, "I'll just leave the situation as it is." On the other hand, you think to yourself, "It's worth the risk. I'll do ask for the raise anyway."

If you choose the first route, you will suffer from the feeling of being a coward. There will be a feeling of underachievement and dissatisfaction. You'll feel like fear has won you over. But if you choose the second option and go into the arena anyway—thus facing your fear— you will suffer from the stress that comes along with facing the fear.

Either way, you are fucked.

So in every dilemma, it comes down to a simple question: What will make you stronger?

Remember that those who are truly courageous, successful, and happy are willing to suffer pain and discomfort in the short run to gain success and happiness in the long run.

Choose wisely.

Chapter 9

The Alchemy of Failure

If you want to increase your success rate, double your failure rate.

—Thomas J. Watson

I know you are one hell of a courageous risk taker.

I know you are because I'm no different than you.

But you see, along the journey you will incur failures and setbacks. You will also witness many things you hate in the world. That's normal. Your reaction to all of that can be one of two—either you feel sorry for yourself and fall into despair, or you get angry. The second option is far better.

There are two powerful forces that run the world and push it forward. The first one is love. The second one is anger. But when failing or seeing something that just isn't right in the world, it's very hard to express love toward this discrepancy, especially when it's fresh.

Here's something powerful I discovered along my journey—when failing or facing something you hate, turn to anger. But not the destructive kind.

I'm talking about a different kind of anger that's based on aggression and passion. Your anger can be used as an ignition for a storm that shatters all passiveness. You can utilize your anger to create a change, move forward, and achieve great things.

Don't be passive; don't convince yourself it's ok to feel weak and powerless or try to force yourself to love this failure or discrepancy. Rather become so angry that you are willing to take the problem by its throat. Turn this failure into motivation for action.

Next you get rejected by a girl, you comply when your heart screamed in protest, or if you see an old man that has to go through garbage cans for food, ignite the anger inside of yourself to take action, and move forward—it doesn't matter in what arena.

For example, one day I came back from an insane cycling session. When I got home, I felt so good I just wanted to scream! I then saw my neighbors, and my lips suddenly locked up. I just couldn't do it... at that moment I gave away my power in the face of fear. That day I challenged myself—and committed on paper—that after my next session, I would scream twice as hard... for this time, and the last one. I was furious at myself, but I committed to fixing this. And I fixed it. I fixed it so well that after screaming the very same neighbors from last time came out and asked me whether I'm crazy... Expressing this excitement was such a relief... it felt so good doing it!

But the point is *not* that they validated how loud I was, or that I showed who has the biggest balls. Rather it's the fact that I took my failure, my slip—which bugged me very much—and turned into something beautiful. This failure served me as an ignition for expression instead of ignition for suppression...

By using this technique you can really embrace with love each and every failure without forcing this feeling, simply because you know, deep inside your heart, that this failure pushed you forward to something better.

Chapter 10

The Path of Innocence

Deep within, you and I are innocent.

Every story you've been told by others and by yourself about who you are has just been fiction. Underneath these layers of conditioning there is an innocent, courageous, true, happy, and fragile person—a real person.

Forget what you think about innocence, and redefine it. Really sit for a moment, and ask yourself what innocence is.

You'll suddenly come to realize that innocence is simply trusting blindly. But you've become fearful of innocence and trust because there's a chance you'll get hurt, so you started rejecting this blind trust from yourself from by analyzing everything and trying to control your deepest heart's desire, thinking that by doing so you will be protected from dealing with pain. But the funny thing is that pain and joy are inseparable. Blocking pain means blocking joy too…

Parents, teachers, governments, and friends taught you that being innocent is bad. "Stop being so innocent; the innocent get hurt the most" is what they'll tell you. But come on; don't you see this pattern? These people are the ones who regard themselves as realists. They are the nonbelievers. They are the people who live a boring, robotic life that has no edge, excitement, or spontaneity… open your eyes, you will start noticing them. And once you do, stop listening to them!

What if Albert Einstein had listened to this kind of people? Do you think that we would have the theory of relativity today?

What about James Watt and the steam engine or the Wright brothers and their plane? If any one of them would have said "Yes, you are right. I am incapable of doing this" how our lives would have looked like today?

There are so many examples to the lack of people's faith—and I bet you have a ton of examples from your own life too. When a person acts with innocence and has completely blind, childish faith in something—be it love, a goal, or a dream—people just come and squash it. And this behavior sometimes comes from the people closest to you. They are simply filled with pain about their own dreams getting squashed, and now they go on infecting others with this feeling as well.

In order to find your courageous, true face, you need to become innocent. Look at children; they blindly trust their own instincts. They're not afraid of the outcome of their actions! That's why so many adventures take place at a young age. That's also why children are filled with so much joy. Kids do everything their hearts lead them to— even if it means putting their hands in the fire or being completely wrong and irrational. No fear of mistake— that's innocence! *That's* courage.

Since being innocent also means—besides adventure and success—the possibility of getting burned, the "serious" people don't achieve 10 percent of their true potential in life. They are simply way too attached to safety and security.

But if you will allow yourself to be innocent, even just a little bit... to walk with faith into the fire, and to be blindly in love with your passions, without fearing the consequences, you will taste and experience the fruits of true courage and joy. You'll taste and experience God. This is not some esoteric idea; just try it. Simply let go of your seriousness for a little while to follow the pure, childish voice that's in your heart and you'll see for yourself what real courage feels like—it's that simple. Ask the questions you were afraid to ask, say the things you've kept behind lock and key, go up to this girl... just do it. The awareness and excitement that come with simply following your heart's desire, without any analysis, and allowing yourself to make mistakes is priceless. It colors your whole existence.

Here's an interesting question: How would your life look if you embarked on 10 percent of your heart's deepest desires—in complete innocence, without any calculations whatsoever?

I know the answer too—one word: *exuberant*.

Do you know why you are so fed up with your life? Because when you lose your innocence, you die. Everything turns gray. When you become "a grownup", you no longer allow yourself to explore and experiment. You settle down into boredom. Into certainty.

And if you really think about it, what's the difference between you and a child—age? Responsibilities? Yes, you're indeed older, and maybe you have a mortgage to pay, but who decided that a thirty-year-old can't just follow his heart, have some fun, and make a few mistakes? You did. You were taught it, and today *you* choose to live by this notion. Every boundary you think you have is self-imposed.

Let go... be innocent. It is simple as that.

Chapter 11

Validation Is the Devil

Validation is a survival mechanism. As little children we learn that by pleasing our elders—teachers, parents, or any other person who holds power over us—we are being rewarded. On the other hand, we learn that by displeasing our elders, we get punished; suddenly instead of ice-cream there's a plate full of steamed vegetables, the ten-dollar bills become chores, and the compliments turn into scolding. So you learned very quickly that to survive and live an easier life all you need to do is to please those around you...

Acting this way was relevant when you were five years old, but now you are fortunate enough to get your own ice-cream. Right now, you are no longer controlled by this notion of "please and you shall be rewarded". No longer you need your surroundings approval to survive, and yet this notion got engrained so strongly into your mind that even as an adult you are very cautious about being an outcast and standing out from the crowd, fearing that without them you are nothing, that without them you will die—which is why the majority of people go on seeking the ok of the masses. But they fail to see this madness; like sheep they follow their shepherd, thinking that without him they will die of thirst and hunger, when in truth they are oblivious to the fact that they have the ability to supply their needs by themselves, without being dependent on nobody.

Seeking validation is a disease, period. Doing so means choosing to be a lawyer instead of a painter.

Seeking validation will make you do everything that the people around you praise just to get their approval, but by pleasing them you will never choose what you're truly passionate about. To be able to express courage and have real freedom in life, you have to follow your own inner voice and *stop seeking validation.*

Think of all the times you've wanted to do something but had this little bird in the back of your mind that stopped you by asking, "What will people think of me?" I know this question ran through your mind a few times today; it ran through mine as well. Every action, no matter how big or small, first goes through this question. This filter. The action gets analyzed thoroughly, and only when you're certain that it won't make you die socially are you willing to act.

But I came to understand that if I choose my course of action according to what's accepted, I will never be able to take off and achieve my goals! How can I? If I'm so afraid of others' opinions and that they won't accept me, how can I go out and do things that challenge the status quo? How can I leave my job, and live off my savings, to write a book if I need the approval of those around me? Man, if I had gotten a dollar for every time people told me I was crazy to leave my job and live off my savings, I would own a private jet.

Listen, people will have something to say about *everything* you do, *every time*. But it doesn't define who you are! Only you define who you are. It's time for you to start living and stop holding back your true desires and potential because of other people. Think about how much courage, power, and adventure you give away when you hold yourself back in the face of this fear. It's mad!

And do you know what the best thing about being free from others' bullshit is? That no matter what they have to say—their words don't affect you in the slightest! Stop acting as if it does have an impact! Even after doing the scariest or most embarrassing thing in the world, your life will simply continue; you will go to sleep, and most likely you will wake up. Your family will continue to love you, your roof will stay over your head, and the sun will rise tomorrow. Shocking, isn't it?

Choose to ignore others' opinions, and do your thing. And if you can't ignore their opinions right now, do your thing anyway. With time, the weight of their words will become like a feather in the wind, a drifting cloud.

Next time an impulse arises inside of your heart, and you feel like suppressing it because you're afraid of others' reactions, go out, and do the thing anyway. Mess it up completely; it doesn't have to be perfect. Going with your instinct is about reclaiming your personal power and peeling away another layer of the armor around your heart—and not about perfection to get everybody's high-five.

Declare now: "Only I define myself and choose what is right for me to do."

And live by this mantra every single moment.

Keep Your Windows Closed

I'm driving back home from some grocery shopping.

Music is playing in the background; I feel great.

I stop at a big junction at a red light.

On my right side, an old silver beaten-up car stops too.

When I turn my head toward the driver, I see that inside the car sits one big-sized man. At first I don't believe my sight, but yes, he's doing what I think he is—he's shaving!

It made me laugh really hard; I mean, seeing a woman doing her makeup in traffic is one thing, but a man shaving is a whole new level.

I looked at him and with a big smile, mimicked his movements, and then gave him a thumbs-up.

The air conditioning was on. My windows were closed.

He looked at me with a face that asked, "What?"

I repeated my movements, thinking he simply hadn't understood me.

I then saw that he was pissed. He angrily signaled me to open up my window.

I could read his lips. He was cursing at me. I guess he didn't like my joke...

This was a very powerful moment for me. I was struck with a flash of insight.

I was sitting there in my car, with funky music playing in the background, and the windows were closed—while he fired what seemed to be everything he knew at me. He craved to throw his poison at me. He wanted to infect me.

But I just kept sitting there, looking at him and smiling.

It was his problem that he chose to interpret my joke this way, but I was not going to partake in his game.

This is a story about not giving a fuck. In your life, for everything you do, there will be people who will misinterpret, criticize, and hate you for doing it. They will try to infect you with their feelings—simply don't give a single fuck. Just do your thing, and give no one the permission to infect you.

People will try to throw shit at you—just keep your windows closed.

Chapter 12

Every Day Is The Day

Death twitches my ear;
"Live," he says…
"I'm coming."
        —Virgil

You need to look at every single day as if *this* is your day, as if there's no other day. There's no tomorrow and no later; it's now or never.

We are being conditioned by society to never speak about death, as if we are infinite. But I want you to think about your death for a moment, and I don't care if you're twenty years old. Imagine what would it be like to lie on your deathbed when you're ninety years old, and think of all the things that you postponed, all the things you missed because of fear; it will feel so stupid that you let fear take you over! It will haunt you! All the adventures you've missed, all the stories you could've told, and all the love you could've experienced! People postpone their entire lives until later, thinking that they have all the time in the world… They don't. No one has that.

I mean, who can guarantee me anything? Hell, maybe I won't wake up tomorrow, so I need to live today! You need to stop postponing dealing with your fears and living your life, hoping for better days or more courage. I did the same, and for many years I ate dirt because of it. I was waiting for these days, but nothing happened; one month passed, two months, then a year, two years… I was rotting away. This day never comes by itself; rather, you need to craft it with your own two hands—otherwise you'll continue eating dirt for the rest of your life!

Start thinking about your death every single day. Accept your mortality. Embrace it. Think of how much freedom and value this fact adds to your life, how little problems suddenly seem! When you really grow around the idea of your mortality, you start thinking, "All of it can end in a second. I have no time to wait!" A person who knows he's going to die has no time to focus on his fears; the clock is ticking, and all of the sudden he starts taking massive action.

Stop saying, "I might ask for her number one day" and waiting for some magic powers to appear—there is no fucking someday. Understand that. There's only now, and every breath you've been given is a gift.

There are millions, literally, an infinite amount of opportunities around you every single day, in every arena you can think of. Relationships, finance, health—I can go about examples for an entire book. *Actually, maybe I will,* but you simply must open up your eyes, understanding that maybe... just maybe... tomorrow will never come.

Start accepting life's invitations, and embark on adventures to the unknown. It's better to fail, get burned, and be embarrassed than to feel regret, asking yourself, "What if?"

When you embrace death, courage emerges like the sun at dawn.

Chapter 13

The Other Extreme

You've been in your comfortable, cozy corner for a while now. It's time to take out the big heavy guns. That is, if you really want to change, of course.

See, choosing to take things slowly while you figure out in your head the course of action to become confident will take too much time. For so long you've been sitting, being passive, and avoiding (real) hard work—just because it was so frightening. You were "progressing on your own pace".

This is over. Now, for a while, you need to go to the other extreme. You need to push yourself hard and do things that you never dreamed were possible, things you had in your wildest thoughts but didn't act on because of fear; approach the beautiful girls you've been so afraid of, tell your coworker that you've had enough of his crappy attitude, dance like a madman in a party... go on a killing spree. You need to put aside your need for comfort and security and get to work—and not just do the minimum but rather go into high gear. Jump into the deep waters; you'll learn to swim inside.

In the other extreme you will discover some things you didn't know about yourself right now. You will taste courage, love, and passion. You will find adventure and exuberance; a whole new part of you will come to life.

After being in the other extreme long enough, when the time's right—and you will feel when the time's right—you will be able to drop both the passiveness and the over-activeness.

In the center, between the two edges, lies the true you. In the middle, you will find that you're not forcing yourself to face your fears and that you're not preventing yourself from facing them anymore—you'll just flow with your heart's longings and only engage in what feels true to you. You will stop being afraid of fear and it will become your friend.

Go to the extreme... you will feel alive.

Chapter 14

The Power of Self-Love

At times, you will encounter mental barriers. It may feel like it's impossible to go up to your boss or talk to a girl, and inside of your heart, a storm will wreak havoc because you don't take action. You want to do it, you crave doing it—you're exploding!—but the words just won't come out. The legs won't move. Your body is locked in place and you feel paralyzed.

You try to force yourself by saying, "Just do it! Get up, and do it, you wuss!"

But nothing seems to work. You experience complete paralysis.

I've been there many times, and let me tell you something—forcing yourself to face your fear sometimes does more harm than good. See, if you force yourself and eventually do it, that's great. You've unloaded your burden; you did the thing you were afraid to do.

But sometimes you will find that even with a gun to your head, the movement just won't happen. That's life. Even the most confident, fearless people experience this at different times in their lives. It's just the way it is...

So we went over what happens when you force yourself to face the fear and eventually do it, but what happens when you force yourself and flake out anyway? Then you are left both with the anxiety that you stirred up inside yourself by pushing too hard and with the anger and disappointment that follow an unresolved matter.

My experience has taught me that in cases where my body is paralyzed, it's best to simply let go. Drop all resistance. I simply start breathing deeply, get my thoughts in order, and come back down to reality. Because, see, the reason you are paralyzed in the first place is that the mind got you in that position with its internal jabbering. At this point—when you are paralyzed— it doesn't matter what's being said; more jabbering isn't going to help!

Imagine a little kid sitting with his father, doing math homework. He doesn't seem to understand how to solve a problem, and the father has to explain repeatedly. After a few times, the father loses his temper. He starts shouting at his son, "This exercise is so simple, why don't you understand it!?"

Do you think that in this way the kid will understand his homework? If anything, he'll understand even less. Now imagine what it would look like if the father were to sit patiently and tell his son how smart and intelligent he is and how much he loves him; in this way, the kid would come to grips with everything his father tried to explain. And you are not different.

So instead of using force and yelling, try to apply some compassion toward yourself at hard times. Tell yourself that it's ok, breathe deeply, release your muscular tension, and let go.

Your anxiety will fade away and will be replaced by courage and clarity. From there, you will have the ability to choose what to do.

Love causes all barriers to dissipate...

Chapter 15

Integrity Is Everything

The quality of a person's life is in direct proportion to their commitment to excellence, regardless of their chosen field of endeavor.

—Vince Lombardi

Your integrity is the most important thing you have, and your words are your commitments. The extent to which you are going to honor your words and respect your commitments will determine how much integrity you have.

When you truly honor your words you promise and speak great things—but you also stand behind these words; you live by them, and act in accordance to what you said or promised. Then, your words become fulfilled; powerful, grounded... no longer are they hollow. All of the sudden you find that this need to respect your commitments acts as a motivator, and pushes you off the cliff to do great things.

Some time back, I was living with my parents. At the time, I was also telling close friends who came to me seeking advice to do big things. I said, "Don't just go out of your comfort zone—I want you to dive out of your comfort zone. Dive into the unknown."

This advice worked great. Friends who followed my advice began enjoying life and tasting the spicy flavor of adventure. I was doing the same, but then came the real test. One day, out of nowhere really, I began considering moving out by myself—no parents, no roommates, no girlfriend.

To tell you the truth, I was scared shitless.

All of the sudden there's rent and bills to pay, laundry to do, food to cook—that's a whole new level of adventure. No more mommy to wipe my butt and cover up for me. I wanted to take the leap, but fear was holding me back.

One day while thinking about whether to move out or not, I came to a decision. I thought, "Nah, it's ok. I'll stay with my parents and move out in a few years, after I've saved up some money and feel more confident about it."

Then it hit me. It was like waking up. Suddenly I recalled what I had been telling my friends: "You must do the thing you're afraid to do—jump, dive, *die*, taste the danger, and live your life."

How can you betray your own words? I couldn't. I moved out a week after I understood this fundamental thing. I was still afraid and unsure about this step, sure, but I did it anyway. Whether this decision was right or wrong doesn't matter; what matters is that I kept my word, my commitment.

It is in moments when no one is watching that you are truly being tested. You need to do what you speak; otherwise your words are hollow. Worthless. And a person whose words are hollow cannot be a man. Value your words... be a man of integrity.

Chapter 16

Shore Ahead!

Coasting is a very beautiful state to arrive at. Only the one who departed into the ocean and had some battles can come back to shore and coast. So when you find yourself coasting, you should first of all give yourself a pat on the back; this means you've been working. You did something different than what you would normally do... you actually worked for a change.

But no one cares what you did yesterday; it's no longer valid today. You can't live your entire life from past winnings! Like a person who lives solely on his big lottery jackpot and has no new income, eventually nothing will be left.

It's way too easy to fall back into your comforting routine of boredom and mediocrity. All it requires is for you to stop working, to lie on the couch and give up. But I assure you that after departing into the ocean of the unknown, coasting and returning back to your old circumstances and life will be comforting no more. After tasting the sweet taste of adventure and its results, sitting passively and letting the days go by just won't cut it for you anymore.

Now I don't care why you are coasting. Family, girl-friend, erection problems, debt, not feeling like working—I just don't care. Get up. Give yourself a slap on the face, and ask yourself, do I deserve *this* shit? Or do I deserve a great life?

I have no special protocol for you to start feeling like working again. I have no magic formula. Coasting in different severities happens to everybody; no one is immune, not even Steve Jobs. You can't prevent it.

The question is what you are going to do when you hit the shore? And since the only cure for this is plowing through the hard times, harnessing your energy and will—are you going to continue sitting, pondering how the magic went away, hoping for things to get better (which will never happen)? Or will you get the fuck up and return into the battle for better life? The choice is all yours.

Coasting has something interesting about it. It makes you feel like maybe you're not a person who can change at all... maybe you were destined for failure... maybe you're trying to do something against nature. But this is the catch: everybody who has achieved something great in his life has felt like this at some point, even the most successful people. Don't let this feeling fool you into believing that you don't deserve to be great or that you were not meant to change your life. Step up!

You must understand this simple fact. It's very easy to lose momentum. And in the same way that it's easy to lose momentum, it's equally easy to create one! Simply come back to work now! Time is of the essence. Do something you're afraid of. Challenge yourself. Step out in faith.

Do you think coming back to work is hard? Do you think that you need some kind of special feeling or words? You don't. Simply shut up, stop complaining, and just do it.

Part 3

Winners' Fuel Is Positive Thinking

Chapter 17

Your Thoughts Determine Who You Are

Whether you are working, shopping, or sitting on your couch doing nothing, thoughts are coming and going. This inner talk you have with yourself is *the most important* conversation you'll ever have in your life.

For years I spoke bad things to myself in my mind; I had a low opinion of myself, judged others, and used negative language to describe everything. And that's how most people live their entire lives. The initial response of the majority of people whenever a picture comes up—"I'm ugly;" whenever an opportunity comes up—"I can't do it;" when they see a girl who isn't a model—"she's ugly."

Our society is constantly looking for the negative; it thrives on it. That's why when you turn on the news, you will hear one good thing for every nine catastrophes. Debt, war, death—the media can go on about it for hours... days... an endless pit of negativity. But how often do you hear about people who achieved great feats, made big contributions, or had some amazing discoveries? Almost never! Now why do you think the media supplies us mostly with this poisonous information? It's not because there are so many catastrophes; I'll tell you why—demand and supply.

It's a vicious, automatic cycle of consuming and creating negativity, and if you continue letting yourself get sucked into it, you will never be able to take off the ground to fly toward courage, happiness, and success. This habit of negativity will drown you!

When you are expressing negativity, it doesn't matter whether it's to someone else or to yourself—in both cases you're hurting no one but *yourself.* Being negative is the real silent killer, not blood pressure. It just seems as if consuming and creating it is such a normal process—so normal that it flies under the radar for people's entire lives! Nobody questions the validity of these infected words, and people just fail to see that this habit, this addiction, is counterproductive, quite insane even. You must start noticing what you focus on most in yourself and others.

Spoiler alert: what I'm about to share with you is old news!

Your thoughts are half of your success. You *know* this already. So why are you still so negative? Is that because positive thinking is considered a cliché by those around you?

If people condition themselves, unlike 99 percent of society, to become healthy and positive thinkers, they will feel confident and succeed in everything they do. On the surface, positive people still might lose or feel unconfident. But deep down, they will treat every event as though they have won—if not the superficial prize, than they won a lesson. They will find the positive outcome in every situation, and trust me; there *is* a positive outcome in every situation.

People come up to me and say, "You went out there to face your fears, you were talking to and smiling at random people—and they sometimes rejected you! Some even laughed and said you were weird! That's not really a success."

Hmm, good point. But here's a perspective I offer these people: Yes. I do get rejected at times. But that doesn't matter. What matters is that I go out, and I deal with my fears—and of course some people don't like or accept it, but my point is to be accepted by myself, and not by others. I measure my success intrinsically, not externally. Now that you know that, do you think I have succeeded or failed?

Winning or losing is all a matter of what you choose to focus on, your perspective.

But the losing kind of people will simply look for the negative in everything. They will invest all of their energy on their failure, how they can't do something, why they're insufficient, and why God had failed them. They continue entertaining these negative thoughts, thus piercing even more the already-drowning ship of their lives.

Here's what you must remember: Actions lead to thoughts, thoughts lead to emotions, emotions lead to *more* actions, and these actions lead to achievements.

And the secret of the happiest, most successful people is: what precedes their first action is *choice.*

But most people believe that what precedes their first actions is emotion. They think that they first need to feel good, and only then will they be able to act. But come on; most of us don't feel like it several times a day. You can't let yourself be thrown off by every little blow. The only way to change your feelings is by taking direct action outside of your current emotion, and thinking pattern. Once you do that, you've broken the chains—you're no longer enslaved to your mood. One action outside of your negative thinking pattern can affect your entire action course during that day, or even your life!

Think about it. Everybody has experienced waking up wrecked and depressed at least once, having one of those days when everything sucks. Now what do most people do? They start acting like a depressed person, and drive people away. They stop doing and fall into despair. "I just feel bad" they'll tell you, and their entire day goes down the drain—life's being put on hold because of it... it's mad! And it's a self-fulfilling prophecy; you let this emotion control you, and the more you let it, the more you find ways to justify your feeling.

Now think about the same scenario, but instead this person thinks, "I'm feeling bad, but I'm going to change it." So immediately he takes action, thinking about how lucky he is to have life, and goes out for a walk in the morning sunshine. He strikes up conversations with random people, greeting them and smiling. Suddenly the person's thoughts start to shift on their own. He starts feeling good, thus achieving more good results. Hmm, maybe life isn't that bad after all!

In conclusion, the first step to positive thinking is to understand and accept that you can't control how you'll feel when you wake up, or what you will feel immediately after shit happens. Feelings float automatically; you can't choose what will come up. Just accept what is.

The second step is decision. It's true that you can't choose what comes up, but after you've accepted your feeling, it's definitely possible to change it; all you have to do is decide. That's all.

The third step, after you've made your decision, is to take action—both physically and mentally—to change your emotions. It's not enough to just think good thoughts and imagine yourself dancing. You need to actually dance! You have to dance, even if you don't want to.

What Positive Thinking Is Not

We all know negative, cynical people. They are the ones who will be the first to tell you that positive thinking is a cliché. The same breed of people will also tell you that they're not negative or cynical; they're realists. Hell, maybe you've even said that!

But reality is subjective. It's true that there are wars in the Middle East; that you have a low level of confidence, or maybe you have some serious debt—but it's also undeniably true that there's beautiful sunshine today, that the grass is green, and that you woke up today!

Positive thinking doesn't mean suppressing and denying your shortcomings and problems. Nor does it mean denying the problems of the world around you. It simply means being aware of them, doing everything that you can to win your battles and overcome the obstacles, but it also means acknowledging that there *are* good things in your life! So acknowledge the bad, do everything you need to do to change the situation (or your outlook about it), and give the good things the stage they deserve while you're crafting yourself a better future. And there are good things, understand that!

Fighting and sweating every single day so that you can come one step closer to achieving the courage you always dreamed of and in the meantime being happy and thankful for every gift the universe hands you, knowing that your life is in the process of improvement—*this* is positive thinking.

But smiling and saying that life is great when in truth you're doing nothing about the fears that control you, and burden you like a big rock on your shoulders—this is suppression, *not* positive thinking.

Start looking for the positive, don't listen to the cynics; they will try everything to rub their misery onto you. And if I found it... you can too.

The Content You Consume

We humans can be very counterproductive animals at times.

One of the things that affects human consciousness, thought, and daily life the most is the environment. As you already know, the things you choose to read, the movies and TV shows you watch, and the conversations you have in your everyday life all have a deep impact on you. Don't underestimate the power of your environment.

If you come home after a long day of work and turn on the TV to watch the news, what do you think you will feel? Will it be gratitude, bliss, or happiness maybe? Not a single chance. You will feel angry and miserable! All of these toxic things flow into your mind, and they stick. They stick like a leech.

But what if you come back home and instead of watching the news you choose to calm yourself with a book that plants good thoughts in your mind? I'll tell you what's going to happen. You will go to bed with those nourishing thoughts and wake up with those thoughts, and the exact same thoughts will randomly appear in your head at the office, at a restaurant, or even during a crazy hour-long morning commute!

The same goes for the music you listen to, the talks you have, and the people you come in contact with; probably one of the most painful things is when people wake up to the fact that their friends have deep impact on their consciousness and understand that although they dearly love each other, their friends simply have dysfunctional thought patterns that make them sick as well.

Imagine a beautiful sunflower, all strong and erect, living in nourishing soil, with the appropriate amount of sun and water, just perfect. The flower has enough space to grow and thrive; it will prosper and give its gifts for a long time.

Now take the same sunflower, put it in dry soil, water it once a month, and let harmful insects intrude into its environment. Do you think that this flower is going to prosper or that it will give its gifts for long, if it gives any at all?

Human consciousness is the same as the flower. So start cultivating a healthier environment for yourself— read books that inspire you and make you happy, talk more with people that you have fun conversations with, watch less news, and listen more to motivational content and less to ranting.

Be wise with what you let into your mind. In no time, your consciousness will come back flourishing, giving you its sweet fruit.

Chapter 18

The Power of Friendship

Show me your friends, I'll show you your future.

—English Proverb

You and your friends act like flowers and the earth to each other. Your friends are the people you can count on and share your journey with. They are the ones who will help you remain on track and wake you up when you start drifting off. Your anchor in this universe. Your lights on a long dark road.

But there is one crucial criterion that will determine whether a friendship is powerful and healthy or diminishing and destructive.

If there's mutual growth, that's a *real* friendship that needs to be nourished and cherished. This kind of friendship is rare and worth holding on to. Anything other than that isn't worthwhile. It's a stick in the wheels, a dead garden; an illusion of companionship.

There are way too many friendships that are based on the wrong kinds of things, such as gossip, prejudice, judgment, complaining, drugs, and alcohol; you must avoid this kind of friendships. Avoid it at any cost. If you already have friendships of that nature, try to support a change with all of your heart! But if your friends keep resisting your efforts, you know what you need to do. You need to dispose of these kinds of people and keep your interactions with them to a minimum; they will infect you like a plague. I know it's hard to do, but some people just don't want to change. Don't let their lack of motivation drag you down into mediocrity.

It is also very important to remember that the real kind of friendship is very rare. So if you have just *one* friend that you can truly share your journey with, you have won the jackpot.

So *s*top looking around, thinking that you need a crowd of five people to feel like you have friends. Even if you have that many friends, most chances are that two of them, at most, are really close to you.

You only need one good friend. That is all.

So I want you to choose one or *maybe* two friends—if you feel like this is the right thing to do—and share this treasure you have found with them. Tell them to get a copy of this book. Share it. Holding on to this knowledge will limit your success.

From now on, this small inner circle will be your brigade, your nourishing soil to grow in; in this circle you will share your ideas, successes, and failures, and you'll be understood. In addition, you will help your friends to achieve their goals, and each of you will flourish. Oh, and helping others is a joy in and of itself...

Chapter 19

Secrets to a Better State of Mind

Give Yourself Some Credit

Your mind can be your friend or your enemy; it's your choice. Most people, as you already know, choose the second option. They'll find something they did wrong in every occurrence. Their self-talk will sound like this:

- "I screwed up really bad! Why didn't I do it?"

- "Man! I should've said that!"

- "Fuck. Now she thinks I'm an idiot."

I bet you've said things of that nature to yourself in the past.

Your mind, right now—in the way it's been conditioned—acts as a spectator who sits in the front row in a football match and screams at the players on the field, "You losers! That's not how you play football!" Yeah, buddy, thanks for the feedback, but it ain't helping. Right now, your mind simply rubs salt over your wounds and makes you suffer for your slips instead of creating a nurturing learning environment.

The people who are successful in life cannot allow themselves to engage in such talk. That's why you must change it *now*.

From now on, in every situation, commit to doing your best. And instead of crucifying yourself with heavy criticism for every step you take, first ask this: "What did I learn from this experience?"

This way you'll know what to improve for the next time. Maybe you slipped—and that's fine—but if you didn't extract the lesson out of the experience, you'll slip again. The key to success in every field of endeavor is to learn from your mistakes.

And secondly, look for points that you did ace by asking, "What good came out of this experience?" And let me tell you that even when you're sure there are no aces in the deck, they're somewhere. Look for them, and don't stop until you find them.

What's beautiful about this approach is that after some time you'll start finding the good that is hidden in every outcome; it doesn't matter how bad things may seem on the surface. Suddenly everything becomes either a lesson or a success, and the term *failure* loses its meaning; no longer is it so burdening and scary to fail.

Also when you actually learn and extract the good from every outcome, you start improving like never before. The why to this phenomenon is very simple. When you punish and judge yourself, you just make yourself miserable. You start feeling bad, and then the only two things you can focus on are your failure and this feeling of discomfort in your body. Your entire world starts falling apart around you; you feel lost. But by approaching things differently, you become objective, and the outcome turns into nurturing feedback instead of torture... it motivates you to be better next time!

You are an ace. And you deserve to be acknowledged for it.

Notice Your Thoughts to Change Them

This method is possibly the most powerful of all you'll find in this chapter. See, because your negative thoughts are so automatic, they fly under your radar. They come in like thieves, deep in the night, and while you're asleep, they rob you of every valuable possession in your house.

In order to change your thought patterns, you must first notice them. So whenever a thought that's dragging you down pops up, say to yourself quietly or in your mind, "Noticed!"

Then start thinking about the things you're appreciative of in your life—what's good about living after all? Be thankful for the meal you ate this morning, the roof over your head, and your health! At the same time, put on a smile, straighten your back, and begin to breathe deeply into your belly.

Now take action! Act in a completely opposite direction to what's going on in your mind. Your action could be approaching a girl—even though your mind tries to stop you. It could be striking up a conversation with a stranger. You can high-five a random person on the street. Anything will do; just get out of your head!

Your performance doesn't have to be perfect! You don't need to be in the most courageous, friendly, and loving mood to act. Even if the outcome looks bad, it doesn't matter. You did something that granted you control over your emotional state, and you proved to yourself that you're not a victim of your emotions and thoughts. Now to me *that's* a win. You'll see that the more *deliberate* positive action you take to change your emotions, the more positive action you take without even trying; it has a snowball effect to it.

Now beware, because the negative thoughts will put up a serious fight. Expect that to happen—but stay a warrior, and keep taking action while focusing on the positive anyway. From now on, the positive wins!

By incorporating into your life this habit of noticing and changing your negative thoughts, you will suddenly realize how much power you have over your mind. You will become so strong, awake, and sensitive to what is going on inside of your mind that the negative will disappear without you even trying!

Some people might think that this method makes people over-think and analyze every thought—that is utterly wrong. When you're driving, you don't think constantly about avoiding an accident, otherwise you would've been too paranoid to sit in your car; rather you're simply being aware of the road, drive with care, and open your eyes wide. And when you recognize a danger on your path what do you do? You simply steer your wheel away from it.

The same principle, of calm awareness applies to the method shown here just as much. You don't need to go about your life twitching and losing your mind, trying to catch and destroy every negative thought; all you have to do is to simply open up your eyes, look to the horizon, and be aware of what's going on inside of you. This is the only right way to apply the method of noticing and changing, because if you become neurotic and live in constant paranoia about your thoughts what do you achieve? The same negativity, just through the back door...

Simply acknowledge the danger and steer away from it calmly. That's all.

Affirmations: Old but Gold

This method is an old one, but I can honestly, full-heartedly say that old is gold. Affirmations have something very profound about them; they are powerful anchors that steer you back into your strengths. An affirmation goes so deep into your subconscious that it plays in your favor—even when you don't think about it consciously. It reprograms your mind and shifts it to a whole new set of thinking patterns, winning kinds of thinking patterns.

To be honest, I tried to incorporate affirmations into my life a few years back, but it didn't stick. It didn't matter how many times I told myself in front of the mirror that I loved myself, how much I imagined beautiful beaches—I always came back to square one. That is because of one very simple reason: all of my attempts lacked something very integral!

Every book suggested to imagine, think, or believe— well, how can you really do that when your body is all closed and shut down after sitting for an entire day, when you're bored to death, and when the smile you put on your face is just a mechanical plastic smile?

After years of battling with these unsatisfying results, I found the missing ingredient: movement. Without movement, without the body being a part of the affirmation process—it's like trying to start a car's engine without gas. You'll get the humming, it'll make a hell of a lot of noise, and clouds of smoke will form, but the car won't go anywhere! In the same way, you can't force a feeling by thinking. You need to physically generate it. I will elaborate on movement in part four of this book, but for now, I want you to *feel* how much vital energy is treasured inside your body; start jumping as high as you can (seriously, get up from your chair!), then breathe deeply into your belly a few times while extending your arms in the air like a bright star, and then shake your body randomly, like a child would... charge your body with energy.

Here is what's going to happen afterward: you will feel energized immediately—energized like never before. If you will feel this way every time after you use your affirmation, how can anything stop you!? This is why you need to combine your body with your affirmations. Only in this fashion will they actually produce results.

Now I want you to be aware that affirmations will create a very powerful, resourceful state of being. But it's also important to remember that they're not magic. Using your affirmation once a week only when your mood darkens won't have any effect; only repetition makes it so strong and impactful, which is why you need to commit to doing the full sequence at least three times a day! After enough time, you will notice that even just by saying silently the phrase you chose to be your affirmation, you can draw up a very powerful state of mind, regardless of the current circumstance.

Also, to really hammer down the affirmation, you need to take action, real action. This is the only way for it to grow roots into you and move you toward your goal. So for example, if my affirmation of choice is, "I can face any fear!" I will do the sequence (the affirmation combined with a physical change) and immediately face some kind of fear. This way I prove to my subconscious that this affirmation actually helps me to take action, and it's more than some cheap pep talk.

So here's our process for creating affirmations:

1. Prepare yourself with two minutes of warm-up. For this step of the process you can put on some music if you want to. Simply start jumping up and down, shake your body and hands randomly, breathe deeply into your belly, and finish with a wide stance, your hands up high, reaching to the sky, and a big smile on your face. With your eyes

closed, feel the joy washing through your body... from your head, down your neck and shoulders, and down to your back and rib cage; feel your stomach filling up with warmth. Sense the energy flowing naturally through your legs and down to your feet.

2. With closed eyes, I want you to recall a moment of true confidence, or any kind of success. Recall a moment when you felt like you were open, enthusiastic, and passionate, a moment when you felt that a God-like energy was present. Intensify this moment with every part of your body, ignite all of your senses; what did you hear? Make it sound louder! What did you feel? Who was around you? What did you see? Make it ten times more vivid! Think of every little detail and get yourself excited as if it's happening right now...

If you can't think of a moment like this, you'd better go and create one; but for now, choose an animal that represents courage and strength. Imagine this beast in all of its glory and feel how its energy flows into your body, sense how this primordial fire fills up your heart and washes you from head to toe, increase the intensity of this feeling... feel as if you and the animal are one, no separation between you whatsoever; let it take over you!

Take a few moments to *really* feel the power inside of you. Make sure to use your body while going through this part—move around with big steps, breathe deeply into your core, smile, shake and jump; this will get blood into your veins, and you will feel alive! Whether you are making something up, or actually recalling an event it doesn't matter, I want you to see the whole mental image through your own eyes—don't be a witness! See it as if you're experiencing this moment right now! (With time, your visualization ability will improve. Repetition, repetition, repetition.)

3. Think of a powerful word or phrase that will encapsulate the exciting image and feeling you drew upon in the previous step. This will act as a cue for your mind to pull the exciting state back whenever needed. For example, my phrase is *I can face any fear!* More examples include the words *power* and *force* or the phrases *I'm powerful* and *I'm a warrior.* Choose something that rings the bell in your heart.

4. Now stop right where you are. While visualizing your moment from the second step, stand up tall and erect, place your feet in a wide and firm stance, breathe deeply, extend your arms with two strongly clenched fists in the air like a winner, close your eyes, smile, and say, "I can face any fear!" (or the phrase of your choice) in a strong, convincing tone. Do this as many times as needed until you really feel the phrase or word is ingrained into your consciousness.

5. Rinse, and repeat! This process takes five minutes tops and trust me; it will give you tremendous results. You'll feel like you can take over the world after doing it. And the most beautiful thing of all is that the more you do it, the more powerful it becomes! After a couple of weeks, when the process becomes a habit, it'll take you two minutes at most

to do it, and you'll find that you start doing it automatically everywhere, in every chance you get.

Taking Action for Someone Else

Every one of us, at some point of our lives, has experienced a stream of annoying thoughts that won't leave. You try everything, but nothing seems to work! In that case, you should do something, and it could be anything, for someone else.

I dare you to try to think negative thoughts while helping someone else. The action you choose to take could be as little as saying good morning to your neighbor and putting a smile on his or her face. Or it could be washing the dishes, cleaning up the house a little, going out to get some groceries, or volunteering to do something for your friend, girlfriend, or grandfather. Maybe you could call your mother and say, for no apparent reason, that you love her. As long as it helps someone else, what you choose to do doesn't matter... I mean, come on; how can you be sad or mad when helping an old lady carry her groceries to her apartment or cross the street?

Really if there's one universal thing that can make anyone happy, it's putting a smile on someone else's face. Try it, and you will see.

Some of the fragrance of the rose always stays in the hand of the one who handed it.

Chapter 20

A Note about Writing

Writing is the most powerful tool to support change. When you write, you signal to your Reticular Activation System (also known as RAS, or in general, your subconscious) that this thing you are writing—be it a goal, a thought, or a dream—is the *most* important one from the pool of infinite thoughts you are having each day; it makes your mind lock onto this thing you've written and search every possible way for its actualization. Committing a thought to paper makes the abstract become concrete. It suddenly becomes real.

To demonstrate the power of the RAS, imagine pregnant women... after they learn that life is now growing inside of them, what's the first thing they starts noticing? Other pregnant women! All of them! Pregnant women couldn't miss a single life-carrying human on the street. A thought, an idea, has become so deeply ingrained into their subconscious that now pregnancy is all they can think about. Now take the same principle... and apply it to having more courage, having a better sex life, or earning more money; writing these goals on paper and really putting your heart into the pursuit will cause you to be just like the pregnant woman (in terms of focus...)—your mind will start noticing every opportunity to actualize that which you set yourself out to do!

Writing also helps you to reflect, get a clearer view on situations, and know what needs to be done better next time. This activity simply helps you focus your attention on what's important and dispose of what's irrelevant.

So start carrying a small notepad around; it's practically invisible. Use it to record your thoughts and feelings about different events in your daily life. Commit yourself to write in it at least once a day at first. Now if you really think about it, committing to writing is very easy; you can take the notepad to your coffee break, to lunch, or you can even write inside your notepad in the silence of your bedroom, just before going to sleep. Spending less five or maybe ten minutes a day on your smartphone is not too much to ask, is it?

After some time, this notepad will become such an inseparable part of you that you'll start writing multiple entries every day without conscious effort!

By writing in it regularly, you'll find that new ideas and ways to improve start arising. Suddenly everything you'll be doing will be directed from a deep sense of purpose and desire to become better. You will become a precision-guided missile.

Getting the Pieces of the Book Together

We have too much input these days, and it's become way too easy to forget things. I bet you're familiar with the feeling of discouragement you get when recalling three days after you've committed to something that you didn't stick to your plan, simply because you forgot.

Now, in this book you've been bombarded with quite a bit of information. If you haven't been implementing the ideas you read by now, you should start immediately. Choose three to four ideas you've read in this book that you would want to focus on for the upcoming couple of weeks.

I choose my goals based on three criteria: areas in my life that need a tune-up, interesting ideas that I've read, and what I believe will be most beneficial for me at this point of time.

Sometimes you'll find very simple things on my list, such as noticing my breath, noticing my negativity, and remembering the three-second rule. The goals on your list don't necessarily have to be grandiose. Little actions done over time create big results.

To actually remember what you committed to, get a small notepad. I use a small, yellow pad of eight by ten centimeters. Every single Sunday morning, I write three to four goals for the upcoming week in this notepad, no excuses accepted. It takes me five minutes at most, and this list serves to guide me for an entire week.

This one single page from my notepad follows me everywhere. It's in my backpack so when I'm on my commute to somewhere, I can give it a glance. When I'm at work and feel like I'm a bit lost, I open it up. When I'm home, I put it on my desk. It's always there.

Even when I'm not reading in this piece of paper, it's in front of my eyes, a zipper away, or somewhere nearby. It acts as a constant reminder to my subconscious that I have goals and guidelines I set for myself to follow. It's like music in the background.

With time, writing weekly goals becomes a habit. At first you'll have to force yourself to remember to take the notepad and write in it. But then after a couple of weeks, this notepad will become a necessary item, just like your wallet and smartphone.

By focusing all of your resources on a few specific goals every week, you are able to achieve profound results in your life. Focus is the key.

After a week, take a quick look at your notepad and observe which ideas and goals were most helpful and which were least. Ask yourself, what didn't get enough attention? What you procrastinated about? What stopped you from taking action? After answering, pick the ones from your list you feel were most powerful, and stick them in a new list for another week. You can also add something new if you feel like it'll benefit you.

Part 4

The Hidden Treasure of Your Body

Chapter 21

The Iceberg

For years I've been this depressed, low-key, subtle kind of guy—and in a sense I still am. That's just who I am. I like the peace and stillness inside of me better than the noise out there.

But there's one key difference between today and my childhood: today I'm happy; I'm no longer depressed. I have happiness inside, and I'm grounded in reality. I do what I love, push my boundaries, and live passionately and dangerously. I jump off the cliff every single day.

But back then, I was simply shackled to my depression and misery, locked behind bars. No matter what I did, I couldn't get myself out of there.

Along my journey, I've also met countless people who are depressed just like I was. All of the people who are in this state tell me very explicitly that if they could, they would change their situations. So if we all want to change so much, why can't we?

When I really decided that enough was enough, I came across something interesting in my little research. Here's also the secret as to why people are so stuck in their depressions and have little control over it. Are you ready?

We stopped moving and breathing!

Look at people around you, and look at yourself! Slouched backs, zero expressiveness, and shallow breaths; it's like people are in coma, doing the minimum to keep themselves from dying, and not actually enjoying the gift of being. This is why people don't just change! You must understand—a mental change is impossible without a physical change.

And this fact applies to you as well, and to everybody who thinks he's not depressed. This is utterly wrong! Everybody these days is depressed in some way—I mean, how can you not be when this vast pool of energy inside of your body is being stuffed down into darkness every single day, disabling your ability to experience joy and causing you to feel powerless against the waves life throws at you?

You must understand that your body is the source of the divine energy. When you start living through your mind—and that's what's happening in today's office lifestyle—your body shuts down. You become worn out and depressed.

Just try jumping up and down a few times, having an imaginary air-boxing match, and dancing in frenzy with an uplifting song in the background. Do it even if this is the last thing you want to do, even if you didn't sleep for two days.

I'm not going to ask how you feel now. I *know* how you feel now. You feel incredible! Your blood is flowing and breathing is deep; you have an uncontrollable, childish smile, with no effort or affirmation needed. If you get a depressed person to move his body this way, it'll be impossible for to stay in his misery!

See we've entered an age that switched from man power to mind power. With that transition, we became sedentary—offices, TVs, and smartphones became the prime concern of our lives. We became attached to our minds, to The Tip of The Iceberg.

Our minds became our prime concern, and the body—the rest of the iceberg—became a burden, a tool! But the mind is just the tip. That's the top, the pinnacle;

does that mean that what's beneath it is worthless? Useless?

Beneath the tip lies a big secret, the secret of who you are... your true nature, desires, and passions. And when you awaken your body, and regain connection to it, you find both a tremendous energy reservoir (physical and mental) and your true self.

Incorporating your body into everything you do, including the goal this book strives to help you achieve, will make the difference between a persona—a story about confidence—and the manifestation of the real courage that is already within you.

To understand your body and its movement, you must first understand sexuality. From now on, I want you to think about sexuality in a much broader sense than simply having sex. A sexual person moves, talks, and breaths freely; sexuality is rawness.

Now humans are very sexual, passionate, and warm beings. But we've neglected this part of ourselves because that's what we've been taught to do. We've been taught that sex, anger, and every other kind of human rawness is bad and goes against society. All of this suppression resides in the mind, in the head, and it affects your body in a very profound way. Suddenly your movement becomes restricted because of your psychology—you're unable to move freely, you're gentle when you really want to be aggressive, your voice becomes softer, and your whole body shuts down.

So when you start working with the body, releasing the muscular tension, and expressing yourself more, you come back to your sexuality. You get back in touch with the source of the divine. When you ground yourself in your body and start breathing deeply, you become more raw and agile; your eyes suddenly have a gleam to them...you start moving like a storm, with fierce intensity, and stop moving like an accident-avoiding robot.

When people feel comfortable with their sexuality and bodies, they feel freedom. They're able to express courage and love and experience real joy.

Chapter 22

Bioenergetics for Freedom

Once we open to the flow of energy within our body, we open to the flow of energy within the universe.

—Wilhelm Reich

Bioenergetics will help you to reestablish the connection between your body and mind. It was founded by Alexander Lowen, a much-acclaimed American psychotherapist, in the 50s. Lowen's theory is based on the works of Wilhelm Reich, an Austrian psychoanalyst and Lowen's teacher.[6]

Bioenergetics suggests that what happens in your mind is a reflection of what happens in your body and vice versa. It also suggests that the mind and the body are in a state of unity at birth, and along the way you are conditioned to separate yourself from your body—thus suppressing emotions, innate desires, confining your movement, and emasculating your sexual energy—in order to keep society's water calm. Bioenergetics serves as a tool to unleash all of these, and it opens up the energy gateways of your body to make you more expressive, flowing, and alive.[7] Using this method, you break the dam and become a river full of life. Bioenergetics creates death and rebirth.

---

[6] Bioenergetic Analysis Website, *Alexander Lowen*
(http://www.bioenergetic-therapy.com/index.php/en/the-bioenergetic-analysis/the-founder-alexander-lowen)
[7] Alexander Lowen, *The Way to Vibrant Health: A Manual of Bioenergetic Exercises* (Bioenergetics Press, 2003)

It's easy to dismiss bioenergetics as some new-age theory because it's something that is, well, a little bit different. It's new. And we've been over this already; everything that is new, that shakes up the status quo, will be considered odd and unnatural.

But in fact, doing these exercises is very natural.

In modern times we've become so logical and scientific about things. We've come to believe that everything has to be concerned with solid information and numbers, otherwise it has no value. Otherwise it is spiritual, new-age mumbo jumbo. So people become depressed; they trust only proofs and science... but it never gives them the peace of mind and freedom they seek. But if you really consider it for a moment, back in the cavemen's times, no one had all of this information; no one was so concerned about the mind! People weren't searching for happiness in offices, nor studying and researching information so much, which is why the body was used for myriad of activities. People were much more in touch with their bodies—they were running, hunting, lifting, and dancing. They were raw and authentic. What you see today is a domesticated, castrated version of human beings.

For me, jumping, yelling, and hitting all seemed farfetched at first, just as they must seem to you. But nothing else worked to help me free my shackled mind (and apparently my body), so I decided that I was leaving all the conventional options behind and going with bioenergetics all the way.

And suddenly something inside of me broke. I became a volcano.

After a while of doing the Bioenergetic exercises in combination with taking action and changing my mindset using the methods provided in this book—again, the body and mind are both equally important—all of the tension that I was stuffing under my smiley face came out. Oh, you know exactly what I'm talking about—this aggression that comes up every single day, in so many situations, but is simply inexpressible! You're dying inside, but the words, the gestures, and the anger just won't come out—and inside you burn in hell's fire. Every time you can't express what's inside of you, the wound opens up, and salt is rubbed all over it, slowly and thoroughly... the pain is unbearable.

Now I have the freedom of choice. When my body gets charged with a feeling, I can choose whether to act on it or not—I'm in charge, and there is no suppression.

Expressing feelings doesn't necessarily mean going all out and hitting the bus driver that pissed you off this morning, but it does mean knowing how to deal with your feelings in a yielding manner. It means the fire is let out; you free yourself and unburden your heart, but not at the expense of the other party involved. This way you can stay free from the burden of holding fire in your belly, and daily events don't cast a shadow over other areas of your life.

You all know the story of the dad who came home after a bad day at work and lashed out at his innocent six-year-old. This father didn't become angry because his child was bad or because he himself was bad; this manifestation of anger happened simply because he couldn't express his discontent and anger in any other way! His inability to express his feelings cast a shadow on his family, and it comes at a great price.

But people who are really in touch with their bodies and are able to truly express themselves will find ways to express their feelings in a yielding manner. They will tell their bosses exactly what's on their mind and will find ways to free their burdened heart without hurting themselves or their families.

Look, without your body you'll never be satisfied. Courage, joy, and love can only be contained in the body. You cannot think about any of these things; they just won't make sense. The only way to really enjoy them is by feeling them in your *body*.

Bioenergetics is what makes the difference between bravery and courage. Instead of pushing yourself through your mind, like a heavy rock on dry land—by being able to let go to the primordial urges of your body and heart, and allowing them to carry you into the unknown, you'll become a leaf on the face of a running stream.

Bioenergetics allows manifestation of the real thing—courage.

The Exercises

Bioenergetics has three imperatives—releasing chronic muscular tension, managing emotions, and unleashing sexuality which is achieved through deep breathing, movement of the body, and expressing suppressed emotions.[8]

As long as what you do follows these basic, fundamental principles, you are on your way to freedom. There are infinite possible ways to apply bioenergetics; you simply need to breath deep, and use your body in a strong, expressive manner, and you will feel the difference between being passive and restricted to free and flowing in no time.

All of the exercises that you will find in this chapter are powerful and should be incorporated into your life.

---

[8] Bioenergetic Analysis Website, *What Is Bioenergetic Analysis?* (http://www.bioenergetic-therapy.com/index.php/en/)

But since Bioenergetics is very flexible, once you get the idea and follow the basic principles, anything you come up with can help you achieve physical and psychological freedom and get the job done. Get creative. Be sure to do the exercises with passion and attention—shallow breath and mechanical movement won't have a powerful effect on you.

First, let's start with deep breathing. It's a spark that ignites a fire, but it's oxygen that keeps an entire forest burning. When people breathe deeply into their core, their bodies are filled with oxygen—they become alert and exuberant. But people whose breathing is weak, shallow, and rigid are like rootless trees. They're all up in their heads—anxious, tight, and unable to enjoy the moment.

From now on, become more conscious of your breathing. Start noticing when you tighten your core muscles, and immediately release them by shifting to full, deep breaths into your belly and pelvic floor, not into your chest. If you take only this one thing from the book, your whole life will change.

Then we have movement of the body. Movement branches out from breathing because only a person who breathes deep has the energy and openness to move completely free... The idea here is to use movement to get out of the mind, become in touch with your body in its totality, and ground your energy.

By being grounded, you feel yourself on the ground you're standing on—you're here, taking part in reality. Most humans are now floating in an abyss, constantly thinking and chasing an endless number of tasks and commitments while being completely detached from their bodies. The feeling most people have in their day-to-day lives is of being carried away by their duties, not being able to grasp who they are on their way. Have you ever felt completely lost in your problems or in your thoughts? To be grounded simply means to be present in your body, to be stable in the storm.

And third is expression of suppressed feelings. I can't stress enough how important doing this is. Each and every one of us carries a load of unexpressed feelings, including anger, aggression, sexuality, happiness, excitement, and love. This baggage of unexpressed feelings is dragging us down, and we must work on ourselves and find an outlet for this force. That is, if you want to enjoy real courage and emotional freedom.

The exercises will be separated into two different categories: "Deep Breathing and Grounding" as well as "Suppressed Feelings and Aggression." Now the separation is just to help you choose better your exercises based on your specific needs and to create order. Each of the exercises, while being categorized, can and will generate feelings that fall into a different category, simply because you can't limit an exercise to do one or a few specific things.

Deep Breathing and Grounding

The exercises in this section are the core around which bioenergetics is built. Breathing deeply, getting out of your head, and grounding the energy in your body are the main focus here.

Exercise 1: Ground Reach

This exercise and the next one are complementary to each other. Their imperative is to induce vibration in the body and deepen the breathing—thus increasing the amount of energy, making you feel more alive and grounded.

Here's what you need to do:

- Stand with your feet shoulder-width apart, and turn them slightly inward to create a stretch in the gluteus muscles.

- Bend your knees slightly.

- Keep the weight of the body approximately over the center of your feet.

- Start bowing forward with your arms, head, and back. Keep your hands straight until the tips of your fingers touch the ground. Let the weight of your head just hang there—don't hold it. The aim is to slowly lower your weight forward while keeping your body as relaxed as possible and letting the stretch happen in and of its own; don't force the stretch. If it's hard for you to reach the floor with your fingers, that's ok; with time your flexibility will become better. Just stretch to the extent you can without pain.

- Start breathing through your mouth, deep into your belly and pelvic floor. You will notice how easily breathing becomes and how your belly fills up with air almost effortlessly.

- Do this exercise for about a minute or two, letting each breath fill you with energy and exuberance. After getting up, you will feel a little dizzy from all the blood that rushed up to your head. It's normal; embrace it until it subsides.

Exercise 2: The Bow

The Bow is a very powerful exercise. After doing it you will start breathing deeper with less effort, you will feel much calmer, and your energy level will skyrocket. While doing this exercise you will find that vibrations and shaking start coming up from inside of your body; this means that the hidden source of life in you is waking up... that an earthquake of energy is taking place inside your uttermost core.

Here's how The Bow is done:

- Take a stance wider then shoulder-width apart, and point your feet outward.

- Bend your knees slightly, and shift your weight forward to the balls of your feet—yet keeping your heels on the floor.

- Tilt your head back to open up your air pathway, and interlock your fingers behind the top of your head (*not* your neck), keeping your elbows as widely spread as possible.

- Open your eyes wide, stretch your jaw open, and start breathing through it, deep into your belly, taking each breath to maximum capacity. Keep doing this throughout the entire exercise.

- Start arching backward slowly; think about flaring out your chest and elbows. Arch until you reach an uncomfortable position—without pain! When your body begins vibrating, and your breath becomes shaky you'll know you've reached the right position.

- Stay in this position, and imagine you are filling a big orange balloon inside your belly with fresh oxygen; feel how every breath you take goes down to your pelvic floor... how your diaphragm and lungs are opening up.

- Hold this position for about one minute. Do this exercise several times during the day; it will wake you up and will serve as a powerful refresher.

There are a couple of variations for this exercise:

- Variation A: Do everything above, but in this variation, tilt your head up, and push your fists vertically into your lower back while arching backward and breathing deep into your belly through the mouth. This variation makes the exercise less strenuous, but it gives great results nonetheless.

- Variation B: This is the full movement. It's very powerful and will induce vibrations almost immediately. Do everything as described in the original exercise, but this time, simply tilt your head up, and start arching while extending your arms backward, spreading your fingers wide, and breathing through your mouth deep into your belly. Don't worry; you will not fall.

Exercise 3: Foam Roller Breathing

A foam roller is one hell of a tool. I used to regard it as some foolish Pilates accessory, but once I got up on it, I understood that this big, blue chunk of foam is anything but a game, so don't underestimate its power.

Foam roller breathing will help you to open up your diaphragm and lungs because by laying down on it your chest cannot elevate when you breathe, which forces you to expand your belly; thus deepening your breathing. It's also fantastic if you have a slouched back and shoulders, as it compensates by stretching your back in the opposite direction.

Here's what you need to do:

- Spread a yoga mat on the floor, and put the foam roller on top of it.

- Sit on the mat with your back facing the foam roller, and slowly begin lowering yourself toward it. The aim is for the roller to be pressed against the area that's between the end of your shoulder blades and the bottom of your rib cage; it's slightly below your nipple line.

- Plant your feet firmly into the mat and start pushing yourself upward in order to elevate your butt to the same level as your back and belly. This will allow your back and head to arch backward with less strain, until your head lies flat on the mat. You might also notice cracking noises coming from your back and neck when you first arch backward—that's completely normal. This sound is just tension that's being released from between your stiff joints.

- Open your mouth up wide, extend your arms to the sides, and start breathing deeply through your mouth and into your core. In this position, you'll immediately notice how easily and naturally you breathe into your belly.

- To get up from this position, elevate your butt slightly higher than it was, and simply push the roller forward, toward your legs. This will allow you to get up from a flat position easily, without overstressing your body.

As you progress, you will also notice that you are getting more flexible in this arched position, which in turn will allow you to lower your butt to the mat and flatten your legs—causing your midback to be the only elevated part of your body. This will create a much deeper stretch.

Today I'm able to hold this position for twenty minutes straight. I like to just lay back and enjoy a good audio book while breathing deeply. It's very meditative and relaxing after a long day of work.

Foam roller breathing is a safe exercise if you do it responsibly. So start with one minute the first few times time you do it, and gradually move upward until you can do it for ten, twenty, or even thirty minutes at a time.

Exercise 4: Rolling the Neck

Since most of the time your head is fixed on screens of different sorts—smartphones, TVs, and computer screens—your neck only needs to move in a very small range of motion. This fact makes you look around and move your head in a very rigid manner in your daily life.

But your neck, which seems to be a very small part of the body, affects you more than you can imagine. Your neck is the root of your head; your neck is the vessel through which the energy that's building up in your mind flows down into your body and vice versa, in complete harmony. This part of the body allows you to experience joy in the body after seeing something beautiful.

But when your neck is stiff, you get locked up inside your head; there's no longer a free flow of energy, so you become ungrounded and fearful, and your ability to be calm and experience joy dies. This is why to release yourself you must first release the neck.

Think about it: you're walking on the street, and you have this invisible barrier that prevents you from simply moving your head unrestrictedly, exploring and indulging in the beauty around you. You're afraid to look to the sides, to throw your head back and see the clear blue sky! A rigid neck locks you up inside your mind.

Here's what you should do to release it:

- Stand with your feet flat on the floor, shoulder-width apart.

- Bend your knees slightly. Feel how your feet interact with the ground.

- Drop your shoulders to a natural position, not forcing or holding them.

- Give your back the freedom to be slouched forward a little. This will relax the muscles around your neck and shoulders and will increase your range of motion.

- Start rolling your neck in a full circular movement. Do it very slowly and thoroughly. Feel and concentrate on a natural, full movement. The cracking you'll hear is normal and isn't harmful. It's just tension that has been locked in your neck joints, and this is your indication of its release.

- Breathe deeply into your belly while doing this exercise, and keep your eyes open—you need to be aware of what's happening around you. Feel your feet on the floor, and embrace the feeling of your belly rising and falling.

- Roll your head five to ten times to one side, then five to ten times to the other side. Follow up with ten deep stretches to the sides, alternating between left and right.

After doing this exercise you will feel very calm, grounded, and much more at ease in your body...

Exercise 5: Grounding of the Voice

The vast majority of people are going about their days talking from their throats. The voice that's being produced, therefore, is very high pitched. It lacks depth. This is one of many phenomena that occur when one lives through The Tip of The Iceberg. You live from your mind, and you talk from your throat; everything is very shallow. Your real voice is a few scales down than what you're used to. By opening up the diaphragm and breathing deeply, your voice will naturally become deeper and more grounded, so basically every exercise you see in this list will help.

But here's what you can do to deepen and ground your voice directly:

- Stand with your feet shoulder-width apart in natural position.

- Keep your back straight, and tilt your head slightly upward to extend your throat. This will open up your airways.

- Open your mouth wide to an uncomfortable position.

- Take a deep, belly-filling breath, raise your heels, and start stomping the floor repeatedly. Every time your heels land on the floor, make a deeply resonating, belly chanting; ha-ha-ha sound. Keep stomping until you're out of air, and then take another breath, and do it all over again.

- Make sure that your voice is coming from a deep source in your core—and not from your throat. Also with every stomp, try to deepen the source of your voice until it feels like it is coming from your belly and has a rich quality to it. Your volume should be high, but not too high—screaming is not the point of this exercise.

- Do this exercise for one minute. You'll learn to feel when your body requires it.

Here is a variation for the voice-grounding exercise. When it's impossible for you to do the original one, you can simply chant deeply and quietly. Take a long, deep breath into your belly, and exhale by chanting with a deep "om" sound. Make sure that your chanting is deep and has a rich quality to it. Do this exercise for one minute. It can be done with a closed or opened mouth.

Immediately after this exercise, you'll notice how your voice goes a few scales lower and your words suddenly become much more impactful.

Exercise 6: Shaking the Body Loose

Imagine what happens when there's an earthquake or a volcanic eruption. The earth moves rapidly; a vibration rises out from the core of the earth. This is pure energy.

Vibration is power. So when you're vibrating and shaking, essentially you're generating energy inside your body. Doing this exercise is also a physical manifestation of psychologically letting go to your true nature. You're letting go of muscular tension, rigidity, and fear to express your rawness and primal energy.

People are embarrassed to shake and vibrate in front of a mirror, even when they're in full privacy. They are

THE BULLET SHIP

ashamed to see their true faces and fear losing the precious, respectable images they have of themselves— and it's exactly these images that prevent them from courageously stepping out into the unknown and starting to enjoy life. I say screw your respectable image.

Here's what you need to do:

- Stand with your feet shoulder-width apart.

- Let your shoulders and arms hang loose; let them float. Imagine every muscle in your body becomes free of tension, as if you're taking your foot off of the gas pedal.

- Now start bending and straightening your knees repeatedly, creating a spring-like motion.

- Create the same pulses in your arms and shoulders.

- Shake every tension out of your muscles without any specific pattern; shake your hands as though there are drops of water on them, shake your head from side to side... shake your entire body!

- Do this for about a minute, until your body feels exhausted.

This exercise is perfect for the morning time because after a long night, your muscles' blood flow has decreased. This exercise will charge you up with some vital, powerful energy and release the rigidity you're holding—both physically and psychologically. Do this exercise every time you feel like you are trapped inside your head and want to come back down to your body.

Suppressed Feelings and Aggression

The focus in this category is on the expression of suppressed feelings and aggression.

You will be expressing emotions from your daily life—such as aggression, anger, sexuality, love, and passion. Everything that was supposed to be expressed but wasn't. Apply the following exercises with your uttermost core, completely surrendering to them.

Exercise 7: Dancing in Frenzy

Have you seen children dancing? They are simply joyous. No other word describes it better. They don't give a damn what you have to say; every problem disappears, and they have not a single doubt regarding their ability to move their bodies.

They dance with all their hearts, and I assure you they're having a blast.

This dancing exercise will help you become a little bit more childish and open by releasing psychological tensions—thus enabling you to express yourself more fully, deepen your breathing, and ground yourself back into your body.

Here's what you need to do:

- Choose some good music, something that creates a fire in your heart and stirs up energy inside your body. Choose a song that just makes you want to get up and dance in a frenzy, to completely let loose!

- Close your eyes, jump, throw your arms around, and sing with the music; be there, fully immersed in the moment. Release everything you have into the world! Destroy the cage that's been holding you. Demolish this dam of energy, and let it wash you with its exuberance. Allow the music to play through you, and let every movement come from your heart.

- There's only one rule to follow in this exercise: let your mind go.

Start dancing like this on a regular basis. Every day take a few minutes for yourself when you can dance with complete and utter joy, and zero judgment. I like to do it either in the morning or in the evening after a day of work. You'll feel alive, happy, and rejuvenated after this.

Exercise 8: Setting Boundaries

We've been over this already; you're saying yes way too much. In this exercise, you'll practice your ability to disapprove and to disagree. You'll be screaming *no!*. Here's what you need to do:

- Spread your feet shoulder-width apart.

- Clench your hands into two strong fists.

- Bend your knees slightly, with your weight directed to the center of your feet.

- Start shouting *no!* repeatedly while throwing your fists down and back in the air and moving your face forward—as if you're shouting it into someone's face. Make this exercise more interesting by throwing your fists to the sides or to the front and by taking big, powerful steps around the room.

- Do this for one to two minutes.

While doing this exercise, you may find that more words and feelings you want to express are coming up inside of you—let them out. Whether you express them by laughing, screaming, crying, or cursing, release the demon you've been holding back for so long.

You'll notice after doing the exercise for some time that your ability to say no has increased tremendously.

Exercise 9: Charging the Legs

One of the parts of the body that is probably used the least is the legs. Besides walking and using the stairs, there's not much you do to use them, so they remain static. Asleep.

But when you awaken your legs, you suddenly become much more powerful. The physical steps you take become stronger, and in turn your spiritual and mental steps become stronger—you become more courageous, directed, and trusting. People who feel their powerful legs have a better sense of themselves on the ground that is beneath them; they're in touch with the earth.

Here's what you need to do:

- Stand with your feet slightly wider then shoulder-width apart. It's best to do this exercise completely barefoot.

- Bend your knees slightly; this will improve your balance and make your steps much more powerful.

- Clench your hands into two strong fists.

- Start marching around the room with a serious face and a locked, direct gaze; slam one foot in front of the other and one fist in the air at a time.

- Make sure your steps are aggressive and powerful. Feel how every step you take fills your legs with blood and energy. Listen to the sounds your feet produce. Think of yourself as if you're moving courageously toward your goal. This is you, practicing moving forward, being aggressive and unapologetic of your courage.

- Do this exercise for one to two minutes.

This exercise is perfect for the morning time. It will charge you up with some aggressive, warrior energy that'll support you to move forward in your day.

Exercise 10: Hand Slamming

Society has become very nice and round. We're afraid to show aggression because the one who expresses it in its purest form will be considered crazy. But in truth aggression is in our nature; otherwise, how could we survive as species? To continue growing, evolving, and progressing—you must start cultivating it.

In this exercise you'll be releasing this primal, raw energy. It will create a storm inside of you; this exercise will wake you up from the dead.

Here's what you need to do:

- Stand in front of a bed, a mattress, or a sofa.

- Spread your feet wider apart than shoulder width.

- Bend your knees slightly.

- Clench your hands into two strong fists—the kind you make when you just want to rip someone's head off!

- Take a deep breath, and raise your arms high above your head—until you feel a stretch in your upper chest and shoulders.

- Using your entire upper body, slam your fists while exhaling in a quick, furious movement—yet naturally, without forcing it—into the surface in front of you. If you raised your arms high enough, you will notice how the movement happens on its own accord without force...

- Yell everything you wanted to but haven't—"I hate you!" "Fuck you!" "No!" "I don't!" "I love you!" whatever your heart calls for—or you can simply grunt aggressively if you don't want to say anything.

- Repeat this exercise fifteen to twenty times. Do it with all the love, hate, and anger you have inside of you. Be a wave; just let the movement spill out of your heart.

You can vary this exercise by doing everything above, but this time slam one fist at a time, alternating hands. This variation is powerful nonetheless; give it a try.

Exercise 11: The Towel Squeeze

You were taught that you need to be gentle because if you use your hand in an aggressive manner, society will collapse, and death will occur. So your hands became physically passive, and now after all these years, you're psychologically unable to grab what you deserve!

Just think for a moment how passive your hands have become. Think about your surroundings, and you'll notice it there too. Everybody is so gentle and cautious about grabbing something. People are afraid to move. Showing any kind of passion or agility is a big no-no in today's culture.

And the hands are an extension of the heart... They're two powerful branches that when given the opportunity will serve as a channel of self-expression and will help you grab what you deserve! You simply must awaken your hands!

So here's what you're going to do:

- Choose a medium sized towel—something from your kitchen will do.

- Take a stance wider than shoulder width, and bend your knees slightly; this will allow better stability.

- Breathe deeply into your belly.

- Grab the towel, and start twisting it. Go to its limit, stay there for a second, and then release the tension.

- Use your *entire* body when doing this exercise; add facial expressions and deep belly grunts to really express your aggression, or use demanding phrases, such as: "I want it!" "Give it to me!" or "It's mine!"

- Do ten reps on each side of the towel. Increase the number of reps as you get stronger in this exercise.

You will notice how aggressive and powerful you feel immediately after doing this exercise.

Exercise 12: The Gorilla

Have you ever seen a gorilla pounding its chest? It's a real show. Have you ever asked yourself *why* the gorilla does that? The answer is simple. Pounding the chest charges the body with aggression and fearlessness; it helps this fantastic beast to connect to its primordial energy. If you'll give yourself the space to experience your beast-like energy, you'll start tasting the fruits of real manhood. It takes some courage to actually let go of self-judgment and shame and go into a cathartic outburst of aggression—but it's worth it.

This exercise will help you to charge your aggression and release the psychological shackles that prevent you from expressing and experiencing emotions in their totality.

For this exercise to gush out of your heart naturally and sincerely, start with a few-second-long warm-up. Loosen your rigidity by doing some jumping, as well as shaking your hands, legs, and head. Feel how energy is charging up inside of your body for your rawness to unveil itself.

After you've warmed up, here's what you do:

- Take a wide stance, preferably barefoot. Shoes are fine too, but they're not optimal.

- Bend your knees slightly, keeping your weight firmly on the midfoot.

- Contract your face muscles, lock your jaw tight, and expose your teeth fully (while keeping your teeth in one piece...).

- Take a deep breath, and start growling. Let aggressive, beast-like growls come up from your belly, *not* from your throat.

- Start pounding your chest with your fists at the same time that you're growling. Your pounding should be stable and firm, but not too painful. Keep doing this until you're out of breath; then rinse, and repeat.

- Do this exercise for twenty to thirty seconds, until you feel an unstoppable flow of energy going through your body. You can also do it in front of a mirror if you want to; it's much more powerful this way.

This exercise is perfect for the morning time. It'll help you get into the warrior mindset for the day to come.

The Bioenergetic Routines

Real results will only come from doing these exercises regularly. And just like you stick to your gym training, you need to stick to this kind of training as well if you want to free yourself.

To make sure you are focused and committed, I crafted two different routines—one for the morning, and one for the evening. The morning routine focuses on energizing the body and releasing the mind. While putting it together, I took into account the fact that morning time is usually limited, so I chose the exercises that gave the best results in the minimum amount of time. The evening routine is less about speed; it's more thorough, it covers a wider range of purposes, and I crafted it especially to deal with tensions after a long day—both physical and psychological.

If you are going to commit to only one of these routines, commit to the morning one; it will have much more impact than doing the evening routine alone.

Note that while these routines include my, and many other peoples', favorite exercises, you should experiment and choose the exercises that fit you best, based on your own tensions and preferences. Also, as you will see, there will be exercises that I did not include in these routines— I strongly encourage you to apply them anyway during your day, and test them inside a routine of your own.

Morning Routine

You woke up to a new day, and what you choose to do in the morning will determine whether you will win your day or get dragged by it. Here's what you must do to fortify yourself:

1. Cold Shower—five to ten minutes

   Just get out of bed, turn the knob to the coldest option, and jump into the shower without thinking twice! After the initial shock fades, start breathing deeply into your belly, and focus on your body's sensations. This will keep you calm and focused while the cold water pour over you and the jittery response to the cold will be replaced by a meditative quality.

2. The Gorilla—thirty seconds

   To warm-up, jump a few times, and shake your hands, arms, and legs; loosen and charge your body for this aggressive exercise. After warming up, take a wide stance, preferably barefoot. Bend your knees slightly, keeping the weight on the midfoot. Contract your face muscles, lock your jaw, and expose your teeth. Now with a deep belly breath, start growling aggressively from your core—not from the throat—and at the same time, pound your upper chest with force. Do this until you're out of breath; then take a deep, full inhale, and repeat.

3. Dancing In Frenzy—five minutes

   It's best to dance barefoot. Choose a song that you like—something that you can't resist dancing to. Turn it on, and lose control to it! Dance completely loosely, with no pattern at all. Wave your arms in different directions, shake your head, imagine you're five all over again, and dance like this is your last day on earth...

4. Meditation—ten to twenty minutes

Choose a quiet place, and take a seat—a bed or chair will do. If you are sitting on a chair, just keep your feet flat on the floor, your back straight, and your arms in your lap. If you are sitting on a bed, cross your legs, keep your back straight, and rest your arms in a comfortable position on your knees. Now start breathing deeply into the belly, and focus your gaze on a fixed spot; let it rest there quietly, without forcing it, and after a few seconds gently close your eyes. Focus on your breath and on the sensation of your arms on your legs. If your mind wanders off, gently bring your attention back to your body. Choose the duration of your meditation based on your experience—for starting out, ten minutes is perfect.

Evening Routine

You've fought your battles, now it's time to unwind. After a long day you must have accumulated some muscular tension and rigidity. You will release all of your fire with this routine:

1. Ground reach—twenty deep breaths

Stand with your feet shoulder-width apart, and turn them slightly inward, keeping your weight on the center of your feet. Bend your knees slightly. Now extend your arms downward, and begin lowering your weight forward and down, to the point where your fingers touch the floor. Let your head hang loose in this position, and take deep breathes through your mouth and into your belly; flood your body with oxygen.

2. The bow—twenty deep breaths

Stand with your feet wider than shoulder-width apart, and point your feet outward. Bend your knees slightly, and shift your weight forward, keeping your heels on the ground. Now interlock your fingers behind your upper head (not your neck!), and spread your elbows wide. At this point, begin arching backward, flaring out your chest and elbows as much as possible. Open your mouth as wide as possible—feeling the stretch in your jaw—and start breathing through your mouth into your belly and pelvic floor. Let the vibration occur; this is a good sign of energy waking up. (After increasing your range of motion, you should extend your arms backward instead of putting them behind your head.)

3. Charging the legs—one minute

It's best to do this exercise barefoot. Take a wide stance, with your knees slightly bent. Clench your hands into two strong fists. Now with a serious face and a focused gaze, start marching around the room with aggressive and powerful steps, slamming each foot firmly into the floor. With each step you take, put one fist in front of you with a sense of conviction. Imagine yourself winning and conquering your target.

4. Vibrating and shaking—one minute

Take a natural, shoulder-width stance. Release any tension in your muscles; loosen the body.

Now start bending and straightening your knees rapidly, creating a spring-like movement, and shaking your body in complete freedom. Shake your hands, shoulders, head, and body; do it randomly, in an ever-changing pattern. Let the movement come from your heart, and don't force it with your mind.

5. Hand slamming—one minute

Standing in front of a bed, a mattress, or a sofa, take a wide stance with your knees slightly bent. With a deep breath, clench your fists, and raise your arms above your head until you feel a stretch in your upper chest and shoulders. Now while exhaling, slam your fists with a quick and powerful movement into the surface in front of you. Add phrases such as, "I hate you!" "Fuck you!" "No!" "I don't!" and "I love you!" Or you can just grunt if you don't want to say any-thing—whatever your heart desires. Start with both hands simultaneously, and after a few times, alternate between left and right.

6. Meditation—ten to twenty minutes

Choose a quiet place, and take a seat—a bed or chair will do. If you are sitting on a chair, just keep your feet flat on the floor, your back straight, and your hands in your lap. If you are sitting on a bed, cross your legs, keep your back straight, and rest your arms in a comfortable position on your knees. Now start breathing deeply into the belly, and focus your gaze on a fixed spot; let it rest there quietly, without forc-ing it, and after a few seconds gently close your eyes. Focus on your breath and the sensation of your arms on your legs. If your mind wanders off, gently bring your attention back to your body. Choose the duration of your meditation based on your experience—for starting out, ten minutes should be perfect.

Part 5

Presence—beyond Mind and Body

Chapter 23

Presence Is the Key

I chose to separate this subject from the rest of the book because presence doesn't belong to any other part; it's not of the body and not of the mind. It belongs to the beyond. It's the meeting point of the cross, the yin and yang; this is the point where mind and body meet, and stillness arises.

As human beings, we've been gifted with a very powerful tool, a tool that no other species known to men has—the neocortex.

It's exactly this part that allows us to have pasts and futures, to think, to be aware of ourselves, and to use language—it's one hell of a tool if used properly. But what happens when the construction worker loses his grip on a jackhammer? Things get dirty. A jackhammer can be used to pave beautiful roads, or it can be used to create chaos.

Now every human being, whether he acknowledges or denies it, has a jittery mind that constantly jumps up and down with useless internal talk, constantly reminding and judging, and it makes you miserable! The mind will even mislead you into believing in things that don't exist. Now *that* is a real mental illness.

Think about it: how many times have you punished yourself over things that were long gone? Thought about what you'll eat when you finish work and eventually ended up thinking about what you'll work on when you finish eating? Or maybe you wanted to talk to a girl, but your mind convinced you that she's busy and isn't interested—just from glancing at her? Your mind is controlling you with nonstop bullshit. It deludes you, and makes you lose sight of what's in front of you. Of what's real.

Currently you don't have the ability to actually be present. And much like trying to hold oil, your entire life slips away between your fingers. You're always someplace else, never fully immersed into reality, and if you will continue living with this monkey-like, unconditioned mind of yours, you'll never be truly happy. The jackhammer has taken control of you, and you are thrown in every possible direction but the right one.

The key to all of your problems lies in this moment. See, when you are present, your mind, which includes all of your fears and worries, is silent. Your body becomes still as well. You're balanced, focused, and you have all the mental and physical capacity to *respond*—not react—in a resourceful manner to any situation.

Imagine it! What would your life look like if your mind was silent whenever your heart called you to an adventure? What if you had the ability to silence your mind so that *you* could decide what to do, rather than having your actions dictated by internal noise and fear? Imagine how much greater your courage would be; this is the ultimate freedom!

Your compulsive thinking of the past and the future holds you prisoner, yes, but I'm not saying that you need to eliminate *all* thinking; all I'm saying is that you need to have a past, but use it for very utilitarian purposes—to learn and for fun, but not to drag yourself into an abyss and lose sight of the reality that's in front of you... same goes for the future; plan, prepare, be ambitious, but don't lose yourself in it.

What you must understand is: time is a fiction. Time doesn't exist. Plant this truth very deeply into your mind... Never was, never will be.

I know you have a watch. I have one too. But can you really measure the past? Where does this past reside? And what about the future? Once a moment has passed, it can only exist in the mind, and that which is yet to come is a fantasy nonetheless. Thinking about your past and future can be helpful, but it becomes harmful when you are possessed and controlled by them, living your entire life through projections.

And that's how people live their entire lives; paying the price of suffering and misery over events that either happened years ago or have yet to come. In both cases, however, their now is simply slipping away through their fingers. And when you embrace the now with every cell in your body, you find real freedom... the mental slavery ceases to exist... you wake up from your dream and finally see the beauty that was in front of you all along.

My goal here is to explain that your mind and your thoughts will keep you prisoner, and you simply must end this slavery if you want to become free. You need to balance the forces and turn your mind into your helpful servant, instead of an emasculating tyrant.

Presence is meditation. With practice it will open the gates to the now and, in turn, to your true nature.

Chapter 24

Fears Are a Gateway to the Now

One thing you'll notice is that even though what I just explained about presence resonates with you very deeply, the understanding alone won't make a whole lot of difference in your life. It'll pass like a cloud on a sunny day—for a while you'll notice it, until it fades away.

So once you understand this simple and important truth—that time is a fiction—apart from engaging in meditation, you must prove it to yourself physically. You must act in a completely different fashion from what you got used to up until now so that you'll see with your own eyes that your past is nothing but a story; it doesn't exist. You must do the thing you're afraid to do.

Every single time you choose to follow your heart, and you face your fears instead of running away, ultimately you're choosing to put effort into and concentrate on the present moment to create a better future, instead of being a victim of your thoughts, circumstances, and past experiences.

With time, as you follow your heart, and deal with more fears, you'll truly come to understand from experience—and not from stories—that there's *nothing* but the present, and your past never held you prisoner. All this time it was your own jail, you're own fiction that prevented you from taking action.

Mind you, it takes time for presence to become a part of you. That is why you must become a warrior, commit to the journey with all of your heart, and plow through the hardships. A lot of patience, no shortcuts, and small wins create big success over time.

You've been giving up and running way your entire life, and it has brought you nowhere. So plow through the hard times, and don't quit too early, or else you will never get to the oasis.

Chapter 25

Meditation Will Set You Free

Have you ever seen a lotus? This beautiful flower grows in the mud.

Who you truly are is very similar to the lotus. Right now, your true self is buried deep inside your consciousness, behind many layers of conditioning and thought. Right now, your true self is like a lotus seed in dry soil. The potential of the seed is there, but it's impossible for it to grow under these conditions.

For this flower to bloom, you must water the ground. You must dissolve the layers that hold back your true power and awaken your consciousness. The key to this lies in meditation. It'll create order in the chaos and separate the true from the false.

When you sit in meditation, you breathe deeply, get in touch with your body, and cut all the noise and interference. And when you cut all outer noise and interference, you are left with two layers.

The first layer is your inner noise—all the chattering that acts like a broken record, and everything you absorbed from your outer environment, from desires and plans to fears and worries.

The second layer is the lotus seed. When you are able to cut through all the noise and get in touch with the second layer, you are with the divine. This second layer is your essence—it contains courage, love, stillness, and peace. The deeper your connection to this layer is, the bigger and healthier your lotus will grow; the more you will be able to express your true nature.

By engaging in deep meditation, you strengthen your connection to the second layer. With time, you'll find that this connection becomes so potent that courage and stillness take the place of fear and inner noise. You'll suddenly find that you have the ability to be peaceful and grounded in every situation, regardless of what's happening on the outside. This is what makes meditation so powerful, and this is why you *must* incorporate it into your life.

Now there is a big misconception about meditation. People think that meditation is some hippie, new-age activity that must be done while seated in a cross-legged position and wearing white cotton and that it can only be done in the woods. Oh yeah, and you need to fast.

That is utterly wrong. The truth is you can meditate anywhere, anytime. Meditation is simply being aware of the self in the infinite stream of inner noise and outside events. So when you notice your body's feelings, your breathing, or your thoughts, you're meditating—and it doesn't matter whether you are at the park or on the train or at the supermarket. Every action, in every place, can be turned into meditation. It's as simple as that.

Now I know how challenging meditating can be at first. Our culture is so active that it feels almost impossible to sit silently with nothing occupying your mind (or hands), but after some time, this barrier will dissolve, and you will find the beauty of silence and stillness.

Imagine your standard workday. You go to work, and the traffic is crazy; cars are honking, people are running, and engines are humming like crazy. This is what you notice mostly when you're on your way to work, right?

Well that and also your thoughts—things you need to get done, reasons you're late, things the boss or the wife said...

Now just think! Picture it! What would it look like if in all of this mayhem you could focus on your breathing, a singing bird, a cat walking silently with a sleepy face, or ants following their route? This ability will give you a peace of mind you've never dreamed of, freedom. And if you're able to achieve this silence in every arena in your life, how can anything stop you? If the mind is silent—or even if it's noisy, but you are aware of it—you can choose your course of action; it no longer controls you! It will grant you freedom.

Not only that, but meditation will also act as the glue that holds together everything you've learned from this book. It'll help you stay grounded and focused, turning you from a child who can't control himself into a sword master. You will turn into the master of your life.

Meditation Techniques

Sitting Silently

Sitting silently is the most fundamental form of meditation. First and foremost, stick to this one, applying it daily. On top of it, apply the techniques you found in the *On Your Daily Life* category when you go about your day.

To do this meditation, pick a quiet place. It could be somewhere in nature, or it could be at home. You need to feel safe, comfortable, and calm in this environment.

Sit down on the floor on a mat or on a bed, cross your legs, and put your arms on your knees. You can also sit on a chair with your feet flat on the floor and your arms on your thighs.

Keep your back straight in a relaxed manner, not extending it too much.

Now pick a fixed spot, something that is relatively small and easy to concentrate on—a hole in a tree, a leaf on the ground, or a black stain on the wall. With open eyes, lock your gaze very gently on the spot you've chosen.

Become conscious of your entire body by scanning the sensations from top to bottom for a few seconds— how your hands touch your legs, how your butt is in contact with the bed, and how your head, shoulders, and neck feel.

Now loosen your eyelids, gently allowing your eyes to close, and simply focus on your breathing. Concentrate deeply on how the oxygen flows through your nose and into your belly with each inhale, and how it flows out with each exhale.

And when your mind drifts off, gently come back to your body with a soft awareness. Refrain from a childish I-got-caught reaction followed by immediately coming back to focus as if nothing happened—the whole point is awareness and mindfulness. Instead become aware that you've drifted, stay with it for a few seconds, and then slowly come back to the meditation.

Start with ten minutes of this meditation daily. If you want, you can do it once more or increase the amount of time; you will only benefit by doing so. As times goes by and your meditation deepens, experiment with longer periods—up to an hour at a time. I can assure you that when you meditate, after a while, time loses its meaning... time is only a matter of perspective.

On Your Daily Life

I'm sure you'll notice that after a while of habitual, deliberate meditation, you will become much more aware and still when going about your day. The awareness will leak into *every* area of your life.

But as I said earlier, meditation is doesn't have to be this Buddha-like activity that requires sitting like a log for days in a forest. You can meditate even while walking, eating, and talking.

So here are three simple things you can start applying from now on to gain more awareness and to meditate in any situation:

1. Notice your thoughts—bring awareness to your thinking process. Start noticing how this compulsive thinking starts by asking yourself, "What am I going to do when I get home?" And like going into an endless pit, you keep falling and falling, thinking relentlessly, judging, comparing, and losing yourself in a fiction. When you notice that you're thinking, it's like catching a thief in the middle of a burglary. The robber just stops and throws away his weapon; he's been caught, and holds no power anymore. In the same way, thoughts will cease to hold you if you just notice them; they will evaporate on their own without any force needed. So whenever you find yourself thinking too much, announce quietly "I'm thinking," and immediately you will encounter a gap of silence in the mind.

2. Notice your body—you should bring more awareness to your body. See, the mind operates like a balloon. If you get too attached to your mind, it will drag you off to a distant land before you even notice. When you bring awareness to your breath-

ing or any other bodily sensation—you come back down to earth. And like a strongly rooted oak tree, you remain in touch with the ground. Start noticing the depth of your breath, the sensation of your feet, the pace and intensity of your walk, and the muscles you're contracting because of stress. Your thoughts cannot exist in the body.

3. Notice your surroundings—this tool is also very powerful. Just notice what's happening around you, that simple. Get out of your mind, open up your eyes, and focus on the world around you! Don't judge anything; don't force yourself to think "This rose is beautiful" if you don't feel that it's truly beautiful; just observe every little detail silently and attentively. I guarantee you will find so much freshness in the old tiring routine of yours! There will be an infinite amount of details that you've never noticed before simply because you weren't looking. If you really allow yourself to dive deep into this attentive observation, you'll be fascinated like a child. You'll notice *everything* around you and become so sharp that thoughts will cease to exist.

Try all of the methods you found here, mix them up, and see what fits you best, and you'll reap the fruits in no time.

Keep in mind that if you really want to enjoy the benefits of these, you must also engage in the fundamental meditation and remind yourself at all times to stay present.

Chapter 26

The Spinning Chair

It's noon, midday boredom at work.

I'm sitting on one of these blue-cushioned office chairs, doing nothing.

I decide that I'm tired of being all corporate and serious and start spinning in my chair like a little kid! Fast!

Spinning in frenzy.

After about thirty seconds, I feel like it's too much, and I stop.

I rest for a while, and do it again.

And again.

But with every time, an insight becomes clearer, sharper.

I spin one last time with full intensity, and then it hits me;

When I spin, everything around me—the computers, the office, the people—they all look like one big blur.

But when I look at myself while spinning in the chair, no matter how fast I'm going, I'm stable. One. I'm not part of the blur.

And in the same manner, by meditating—this is what I feel in my life. My roots grow deep into the ground, making *me* so present and stable, that everything outside of my being becomes just one big blur. I get in touch with the divine, and it makes me understand how nothing but it exists... how fleeting is everything... how nothing and no one has power over my being, and that all of my fears and thoughts are just an illusion... I can suddenly tell the difference between what is important and unimportant. I become still minded, and great freedom follows it.

Part 6

Sustaining the Empire

Chapter 27

Quit Now!

"Quit the wrong stuff.
Stick with the right stuff.
Have the guts to do one or the other."
    —Seth Godin, The Dip

They say successful people never quit. This is wrong. Successful people quit all the time—they just have the balls to admit they were wrong, that their current courses of action didn't get them the results they wanted, and they're willing to sweat, and change. So I'm asking you right now, do you have the balls to admit you're wrong and start working toward a change? Are you willing to bust your ass toward a change? Becoming a warrior, grabbing the sword, and going into the arena?

This is it; the book is coming to its end. It's time to actually get to work and quit the bullshit. If you *really* want to succeed on your way to courage and freedom, you must sacrifice some things in your life. You must quit the things that hold you back in the past, and create a better future for yourself. You deserve it.

For me, becoming free required quitting my laziness. I came to realize that I liked being lazy. It was convenient! Being lazy meant living the lousy life I'd created and doing nothing to change it. Such a cozy, easy outlet... So at some point, I had to face a serious question: Was I willing to quit the shitty excuses and change my life for good? And the answer, of course, was yes. I was so fed up, so exhausted and hateful toward my life, that I was willing to pay the real price; not money, but pain.

See, all of us face this unwillingness to pay the price on one level or another. You talk to a fat person, and he tells you, "Yeah, of course I want to be ripped." But he's not serious enough about changing; he wants it, but he won't quit comfort to get it. He might tell you otherwise, but the donuts and mediocrity are more important to him than getting ripped.

So the questions you need to ask yourself in regard to achieving courage and freedom are, what's holding you back? And are you willing to quit it to start changing your life *today*?

Like I said before, every time you choose to deal with the question or problem head on, with a clear decision, instead of running away and suppressing it, you choose to be a man who appreciates the present and refuse to be a victim of your circumstances and past experiences. Oh, and believe me, I've met some people with hard, brutal stories, and they did it; they changed their lives. I did it. So can you.

Quit what's holding you back *now*.

Chapter 28

Your Ultimate Mission

You have been chosen. I'm dead serious.

Since you've been so fed up with your situation that you actually went out to seek guidance and got this book, you now have a mission. You've been chosen to change the world.

Your first mission is to help yourself. You need to make a change in your life, set yourself free from mental slavery, and expose your true face—only then will you be able to help others.

But it doesn't stop with changing your life. See, we live in a world with other humans, some of whom don't have the gift of access to the truth you've found in this book. Not because it's impossible to get it but because people think they can't change, that they don't have what it takes. Some have completely lost faith and stopped even hoping for a change.

Because you believe otherwise, your ultimate mission from now on is to pay it forward. Understand that paying it forward, and pushing people toward change doesn't necessarily require you to write a book; all you have to do is be courageous, do what's in your heart, and take leaps of faith—because when you set yourself free, you give other people the permission to do the same. Also, spread your knowledge, share your experience... sometimes a single word can push a person to take a life changing step. It's that simple! Remind those around you that's it's possible! Real change begins with small, seemingly insignificant actions, but like ripples on the face of the ocean, they go very far... Never underestimate the power of one, never think that you are powerless in helping others, and never think that you need to do something extreme to change someone's life. By changing your life for the better and becoming courageous , you are affecting every human being that is around you. *That's* how you change the world.

Look, you and I are not alone in this universe. You will see that although the achievements and gains from everything you do for yourself will be amazing, they're all fleeting—eventually they become just another thing...

I've found that real joy, real pleasure, real *love* come ten times stronger when I help other people do what's in their hearts. Because what other reason is there for our existence? We came to this universe to enjoy our lives, definitely, but above all we are here to leave it in a better condition than the one we received it in.

Helping others puts so much joy in my heart that goose bumps rush through my skin, and sometimes even tears come to my eyes when I see what I helped to achieve. Divinity is what you will feel when you come from a place of giving and having a mission on this earth. And the best part of coming from this place is that when you *really* give with love, and give for the sake of giving without asking for anything in return, you get back ten times more than what you've expected.

You have a mission on this earth; show them that it's possible.

Afterword

After reading a great book, I frequently find myself asking how this author was able to generate this beautiful thing. Where did it come from?

The how was never clear to me. I knew that there were places where you could learn writing, but no one could really teach you *what* to write.

And then one day, I decided that I was going to write my own book. I had no idea how I was going to do it. I just knew what it was going to be about and that I had to do it—I would either write it or die trying. It's sink or swim for me in every area I approach; I'm this extreme.

And so my journey began. I knew that I had taken something big upon myself, something bigger than I had ever committed myself to before. But I knew I had what writing this book would take. I had the knowledge, the experience, and, above all, the willingness to do everything to succeed.

As I began writing, this book took on a life of its own. It started with responsibility and courage, and from there the words just kept gushing out of me; with every page I wrote, I found out how much I've experienced and learned along my journey. This fact made me wonder; all these years I had been giving only a fraction of what I had to the world—without even realizing I had so much more in my tank. And if I'm no different than any other person, then what do others have to give that they hold back? What will others take to their graves because of fear and self-doubt?

This book has been a blessing to me. It pushed me out of my comfort zone countless times; I knew that if I told my readers to do something, I must do it too. As you were faced with hard questions, I too had to answer them. I was juggling many tasks on top of writing this book, and one questions led me to this answer: I had to leave my job, which represented my decision to take this book one step further and to dedicate myself fully to the making process. I sincerely hope that you also gave some tough answers in such a manner that shook your life to its core.

I believe we tend to share our goals way too much, which makes us lose motivation prematurely. After hearing so many opinions and words of advice, even the most confident, stable person falls into confusion and starts to question his chosen path. And since I'd made this mistake many times, I decided that this time, I needed to be targeted. I needed silence's fire to guide me through my path all the way to the finish line, to think and create. That's why this book has been a secret; nobody, and I mean *nobody*, knew that I was writing it. I decided to keep it a secret until it was out in the open, which meant that my family, friends—everybody—were in the dark for a long time, and trust me, keeping things this way was *hard*. Writing this book was *my* solo journey—and while nobody was a part of it, everybody was a part of it.

Sometimes along the way, I had no clue what to do, and I felt lost and tired, but I had a clear vision of what the outcome should be, and above all, I was willing to risk and make mistakes, which made my creativity go sky high and made problem solving easier. When you're not afraid of failure, your heart blooms...

This book has been written out of my own experienced pain and through the pain of others. I cried, sweated, and worked hard, but I would never trade my way for anything else in the world.

At the beginning of this book, you wrote a commitment to yourself—come back to it often, and remind yourself why you're doing what you're doing, because in the why lies the fire to move forward. And when the fire doesn't feel strong enough to push you forward—harness your will, and keep going anyway, like a warrior.

Fulfill your commitment by living courageously, and stop running away from your fate. Changing your life is painful, it's hard, and it feels lonely at times, but at the end of the day, when the lights are off and you're lying in your bed, the deepest sense of integrity will wash over your body—nothing in this world is better than that feeling. And always remember, doesn't matter how hard things may seem, or how bad you've been hit; this too will be over...

Now you're not alone, so spread the word for those who are, and little by little, the people around you will start to blossom too. Don't let anybody tell you that it's impossible to change the world!

I am full of gratitude to you for reading this beautiful book.

Yours sincerely, Roi Ostrovsky

Visit the Site

Visit www.roi.pub now, and get instant access to many more resources, including:

- a powerful list of books;
- articles;
- Q&A's section
- and much more.

Take advantage of these resources, and start living courageously today.

www.roi.pub

References

Introduction

1. Cohelo, Paulo. *The Alchemist.* New York: HarperCollins Publishing, 1993.

2. Shedd, John A. *Salt from My Attic.* Portland: Mosher Press, 1928.

Part One

3. Emerson, Ralph Waldo. *Essays: First Series, Compensation.* 1841.

4. McCandles, Christopher Johnson. *Excerpt from a letter.* South Dakota: 1992.

5. Cohelo, Paulo. *Veronika Decides To Die.* New York: Harper Perennial: 2006.

Part Four

6. International Institute for Bioenergetic Analysis Web. *Alexander Lowen.* 5 Nov 2017. (http://www.bioenergetic-therapy.com/index.php/en/the-bioenergetic-analysis/the-founder-alexander-lowen)

7. Lowen, Alexander. *The Way to Vibrant Health: A Manual of Bioenergetic Exercises.* Bioenergetics Press: 2003.

8. International Institute for Bioenergetic Analysis Web. *What Is Bioenergetic Analysis?. 5 Nov 2017.* (http://www.bioenergetic-therapy.com/index.php/en/)

www.ingramcontent.com/pod-product-compliance
Lightning Source LLC
LaVergne TN
LVHW051239080426
835513LV00016B/1672